The Fortuitous Teacher

CHANDOS
INFORMATION PROFESSIONAL SERIES

Series Editor: Ruth Rikowski
(email: Rikowskigr@aol.com)

Chandos' new series of books is aimed at the busy information professional. They have been specially commissioned to provide the reader with an authoritative view of current thinking. They are designed to provide easy-to-read and (most importantly) practical coverage of topics that are of interest to librarians and other information professionals. If you would like a full listing of current and forthcoming titles, please visit www.chandospublishing.com.

New authors: We are always pleased to receive ideas for new titles; if you would like to write a book for Chandos, please contact Dr Glyn Jones on g.jones.2@ elsevier.com or telephone +44 (0) 1865 843000.

The Fortuitous Teacher

A Guide to Successful One-Shot Library Instruction

Sarah Cisse

Nova Southeastern University, USA

ELSEVIER

Amsterdam • Boston • Cambridge • Heidelberg
London • New York • Oxford • Paris • San Diego
San Francisco • Singapore • Sydney • Tokyo
Chandos Publishing is an imprint of Elsevier

CP

CHANDOS
PUBLISHING

Chandos Publishing is an imprint of Elsevier
50 Hampshire Street, 5th Floor, Cambridge, MA 02139, USA
The Boulevard, Langford Lane, Kidlington, OX5 1GB, UK

Notices
Knowledge and best practice in this field are constantly changing. As new research and
experience broaden our understanding, changes in research methods, professional practices,
or medical treatment may become necessary.

Practitioners and researchers must always rely on their own experience and knowledge in
evaluating and using any information, methods, compounds, or experiments described
herein. In using such information or methods they should be mindful of their own safety
and the safety of others, including parties for whom they have a professional responsibility.

To the fullest extent of the law, neither the Publisher nor the authors, contributors, or
editors, assume any liability for any injury and/or damage to persons or property as a
matter of products liability, negligence or otherwise, or from any use or operation of
any methods, products, instructions, or ideas contained in the material herein.

British Library Cataloguing-in-Publication Data
A catalogue record for this book is available from the British Library

Library of Congress Cataloging-in-Publication Data
A catalog record for this book is available from the Library of Congress

ISBN: 978-0-08-100193-6 (print)
ISBN: 978-0-08-100240-7 (online)

For information on all Chandos Publishing publications
visit our website at https://www.elsevier.com/

Working together
to grow libraries in
developing countries

www.elsevier.com • www.bookaid.org

Publisher: Glyn Jones
Acquisition Editor: Glyn Jones
Editorial Project Manager: Harriet Clayton
Production Project Manager: Debasish Ghosh
Designer: Greg Harris

Typeset by TNQ Books and Journals

This book is dedicated to all of the students I have taught, for the many great lessons they have taught me.

CONTENTS

ABOUT THE AUTHOR

Sarah Cisse is a Reference and Instructional Librarian II at the Alvin Sherman Library Research and Information Technology Center at Nova Southeastern University (NSU). She received her Master of Information and Library Science (MILS) degree at Pratt Institute in 2005. Sarah began her library career at the Metropolitan College of New York as an Information Specialist. Previous experience includes positions as Information Assistant in the Museum at the Fashion Institute of Technology (MFIT) and as Records Manager at the New York City (NYC) Department of Consumer Affairs. Sarah also holds a B.A. degree in English Literature and an A.A.S. degree in Advertising and Marketing Communications. She has over 15 years of experience in the library science and museum field combined. This includes local and distance instruction, creating online resource tools, program planning, reference, collection maintenance, records management, and cataloging. She has served on several NSU Libraries committees and 3 years on the Southeast Florida Library Network (SEFLIN) conference planning committee.

PREFACE

This book is about the academic librarian as teacher, how Master of Library Science (MLS) programs prepare academic librarians to teach, and how they gain practical teaching experience on the job. Through collaboration with teaching faculty, the one-shot instruction session remains a fixture in academic library instruction. In light of this reality, academic librarians seek practical tips to create successful one-shot sessions.

Although academic library instruction has a long history, its roots can be traced only as far back as Germany in the seventeenth century. Evidence of library instruction was found at Harvard College as early as the 1820s. However, the history of modern library instruction began in 1876 when Melvil Dewey urged librarians to become educators. Academic librarians in the United States began teaching in classrooms and writing about it in the late nineteenth century. In the 1880s, some academic librarians were already lecturing in the classroom. In fact, between 1876 and 1910, 60 universities were offering library research instruction in various formats.

The term bibliographic instruction (BI) is a relatively modern construct, and its short history as a professional area of concern in the information field spans three decades. The 1970s viewed BI as library orientation; the 1980s saw the development of ideas and methods of bibliographic instruction and a growing trend toward defining BI as a way of teaching patrons how to research resources. During the 1980 and 1990s, librarians reflected on the meaning and complexity of Information Literacy (IL), its competencies, how people learn them, and how they are taught. The concept evolved over those two decades, and, during the 1990s, librarians struggled to understand and communicate the notion, scope, and boundaries of IL. By the new millennium, with the emergence of new information technologies, the development of academic library instruction was greatly impacted. Today, the consensus is growing that IL and its related competencies, such as media and digital literacy, critical thinking ability, ability to engage in lifelong learning, and problem-solving ability, are essential for individual and community empowerment, workforce readiness, and global competitiveness.

The work of the academic instruction librarian has changed drastically over time. Much has been written by librarians themselves about how their job responsibilities have changed since the nineteenth century. The academic librarian of the 1800s was usually a professor, partially responsible for the library. Gradually the image of the academic librarian changed from a service professional simply waiting for questions and giving back searches with minimal input, into one in which the academic librarian is a part of a team of information gatherers, selecting and evaluating information in advance. Despite these major transformations, many still express a need for the role of academic librarian to be regarded as visible, vital, and collaborative within their institutions and the communities they serve.

This book also addresses classroom dynamics and culture, how to gain faculty buy-in, engaging student interest, and practical tips for one-shot instruction sessions. These are all wise considerations for creating successful academic instruction sessions.

Although there are books about academic library instruction and tips for teaching, these volumes do not fully address how current MLS programs are preparing librarians to teach, and specific ways for librarians to gain practical teaching experience. Thus, the book intends to fill a gap in the literature.

The main intention was to produce a book that provides practical teaching advice for new librarians and MLS students, and to provide information about the history and future of library instruction. The book covers pedagogical theory as well as practical advice, with each chapter including a mix of current and future practices in academic library instruction. The target audience includes practitioners, library science students, and those interested in the library science field. The work is designed to have a practical appeal.

I hope that this book will provide useful advice for conducting one-shot instruction sessions, promote an understanding of academic library instruction, and facilitate the creation of successful academic library instruction.

Sarah Cisse
Fort Lauderdale, USA
August 2015

CHAPTER 1

The Academic Librarian as Teacher

1.1 TRADITIONAL AND CHANGING ROLES OF THE ACADEMIC LIBRARIAN

If you ask any academic librarian today, they would most likely agree that the role of the librarian has changed drastically over the last century. Much has been written by librarians themselves about how their job responsibilities have changed over the last two centuries. As early as 1840, Ralph Waldo Emerson encouraged colleges to appoint a "professor of books" with the statement that a faculty position such as this was urgently needed. In the last three decades of the 19th century, librarians repeatedly referred to this statement as a rationale for library skills and reference instruction (Tucker, 1980).

The academic librarian of the 1800s was usually a professor, partially responsible for the library. This professor may have been chosen for the position because of his or her generalist interests or maybe a natural inclination to teach the use of library materials for academic purposes. However, many of these professor–librarians were being pushed from the teaching role by the responsibility of rapidly growing collections (Hopkins, 1982).

The traditional academic library setting, with book collections all around, has never been seen as comfortable for work or study (Bridges, 2001). The academic librarian is pictured as waiting for questions and giving back searches with minimal input. This image has slowly transformed into one in which the academic librarian is a part of a team of information gatherers, selecting and evaluating information in advance (Helfer, 1997). For a long time the library and information science (LIS) profession has been concerned with its image. In light of major changes in the field of information science, the restructuring of higher education, the increased competition between information

The Fortuitous Teacher
ISBN 978-0-08-100193-6

providers, and the new conditions under which information organizations operate, the professional librarian's image is always a concern. In today's information-driven world, the question of how the library and librarians are perceived is even more significant (Vassilakaki & Moniarou-Papaconstantinou, 2014).

The image of the librarian is inextricably tied to the image of the library. Ellis and Phillips (2013) felt that the library as a physical space has been impacted by social constructivism, which has dictated its role and design as an informal teaching and collaborative learning space on campus. Increasingly, library spaces are being recognized as casual learning spaces which may need to be not only redesigned but also reconceptualized to best meet the needs of students. This has been a primary initiative in many recent library redevelopments, evident in many innovative projects. These projects usually focus on library teaching spaces designed for flexible group work, small-group collaboration, individual study, and formal teaching. Some of these redevelopments have included attempts to transform library service areas from the traditional separate circulation and reference desk to a single service point. Social constructivism has impacted the redesign of student spaces in libraries, but has had less impact on service point design and delivery.

Despite these major transformations, many have expressed a need for the role of academic librarian to be regarded as visible, vital, and collaborative within their institutions and the communities they serve. Academic librarians want to be considered as essential to the enterprise and activities of their organization; as well as valued for their contribution to quality education. Specifically, they recognize the need to create and carry out their role as instructor, which is an increasingly essential part of academic librarianship (Ellis & Phillips, 2013).

Some feel that academic librarians need to move beyond the limiting nature of bibliographic instruction (BI) to a more comprehensive concept of instruction, embracing a much broader and more integrated role compared to the passive nature of reference desk service in which professionals wait for the user to determine the question and then decide to ask it. Beyond the academic reference desk, library instruction has always meant more than simply giving tours of the library or fulfilling faculty requests for instruction of bibliographic sources to a class. Teaching in the academic library included an outreach mind-set, in which librarians determined the various information needs of the user community, designed custom instruction sessions, and presented them in a variety of formats and locations to meet those needs (Creth, 1995).

In 1978, Lynch wrote that the main objective of library instruction has always been to empower users to use libraries effectively throughout their lives. Academic librarians, through library skills programs and instruction, identify objectives and design programs to meet those objectives. Often this can be a frustrating endeavor if the institution itself has not recognized or articulated the goal or objective that the library program is designed to achieve.

These frustrations did not disappear when the variety of instructional formats grew exponentially with the advent of online education and electronic resources. Academic librarians were tasked with motivating and building confidence in students' ability to effectively use these electronic resources. Academic librarians also had to improve their own skills with computers and electronic resources. In addition, and at the same time, they had to work to minimize technical problems during teaching with electronic resources to reduce negative effects on both student and faculty confidence (Lynch, 1978).

Academic librarians instructing during this time of transition found that it was very easy for students and faculty to revert to old familiar ways of doing research. General suspicion of and resistance to the use of computers posed a steep learning curve for many students and faculty at the time. Academic librarians tried to avoid anything that may overwhelm students, such as a long list of databases and difficult search techniques, and instead focused on teaching the techniques that address their immediate research needs. Strategies such as these helped build student confidence and an interest in learning techniques that were more advanced when using electronic resources (Shen & Gresham, 2000).

Academic libraries made the transition to online instruction quite early in the overall migration of education to web-based environments. They were among the first pioneers in delivering information through electronic means, which usually included providing electronic guides to accompany those early electronic interfaces. So for academic libraries and librarians, delivering instruction online is nothing new, but what has fast become commonplace is the delivery of the entire instructional experience through electronic means via distance or online learning programs (Allen, 2008).

Goetsch (2008) reminisced about the kind of professional librarian work that was done 25 years ago or more. As a reference librarian, she worked on a desk for about 20 h per week, using a print reference collection and a first-generation automated circulation system. She taught BI sessions with an overhead projector to show students resources such as sample pages from the Readers Guide to Periodical Literature and the library's green-bar serials holdings list. Her exposure to computers and automation in library school was limited to an assignment using an online computer library catalog (OCLC) "beehive" terminal and another using punch cards and a knitting needle, as well as conducting a search in DIALOG, a predecessor to the world wide web, to fulfill a course requirement.

Despite this, Goetsch, like most reference librarians, had to master the transition from print to electronic resources, along with going from mediating those resources on behalf of the user through online search services, to helping users on site and remotely with a vast amount of electronic information. Academic librarians have had to become increasingly technologically literate, incorporating some of the skill sets of a systems or information technology librarian, as information and productivity tools have come together on the desktop computer (Goetsch, 2008).

So academic librarians have had to learn new skills and set priorities in relation to other more traditional reference activities to have the time and energy to move into the knowledge management enterprise. Academic librarians with knowledge of information organization and electronic resources were highly qualified to act as partners in creating the current online electronic resources environment (Creth, 1995).

Ogunsola (2011) feels that the rapid development of online electronic resources has caused libraries worldwide to make great changes in both their collections and their service structure. Libraries went through a major transformation from a manually to a technologically driven system. Although the changes in libraries and the role of librarians originated in the US and other English-speaking countries, because electronic networks do not have geographical boundaries their impact has spread rapidly. With the global reach of Internet networks, access to traditional library services is now available to those who would like the opportunity to attain information about all subjects, free of political censorship.

Today, academic librarians across the globe have taken on the role of educator to teach users how to find information not only in the library, but through these networks. Traditional academic libraries and librarians exist alongside electronic libraries, which some feel could erode the functions of both. However, others would argue that both traditional academic libraries and librarians must remain on the scene. The role of academic librarian can remain relevant if they reeducate themselves as information managers, with the ability to sift, evaluate, and filter the information available through electronic resources and on websites (Ogunsola, 2011).

Academic librarians have also had to expand their presence in online course development and delivery in a meaningful way. Initially, online library instruction used the traditional reference model, but this has evolved in that academic librarians are usually integral members of course development teams and commonly function as instructors in the online environment. In the early years of librarian participation in the virtual campus environment, the focus was often on a single program or course. This has shifted such that online library resources are usually available to all distance users of a college or university. Academic librarians collaborate with college web developers to ensure that content, particularly online library resources, is effectively presented to distance learners. In this way, the role of the academic librarian has expanded to include acting as research consultants, reference points, collection development selectors, and as instructors in their "everyday" role on campus, as well as online (Shepley, 2009).

With the shift to an online learning environment, some feel that the future of academic libraries is uncertain with the ongoing thinning of print collections and continual construction of classrooms, computer labs, writing centers, or student lounges in their place.

Physical libraries are expected to be a thing of the past. The only tool one may need is an electronic mobile device with Internet access allowing one to retrieve all types of information. The development of information literacy (IL) initiatives has emphasized that the traditional role of the academic librarian must now include instruction or teaching. With these initiatives traditional user education methods such as library orientation, library instruction, and BI have also gradually changed. Academic librarians today are expected to act beyond the traditional role of acquiring, organizing, disseminating, and preserving information. They are charged with educating users in how to effectively and efficiently retrieve, evaluate, and use online information, in addition to fulfilling their traditional roles (Wickramanayake, 2014).

With these changes in mind, some academic librarians are reexamining their academic professional role and considering options such as teaching full semester credit-bearing courses. Some are thinking beyond IL instruction and collaborative teaching and are considering teaching in their own field of specialization or maybe a university core course, possibly joining the ranks of the teaching faculty on campus. Although academic librarians have always taught, even while assisting patrons in the library, they may want to consider expanding this aspect of their profession to fully take command of the classroom (Loesch, 2010).

1.2 HOW DO LIBRARY SCIENCE PROGRAMS PREPARE ACADEMIC LIBRARIANS TO TEACH?

In 1978, Toy et al., wrote that the curricula of library schools have always had a tendency to ignore the increasingly significant activity of formal classroom teaching within the profession. Even today, some library schools have courses in classroom techniques; however, many graduates do not have any training in the process of organizing, developing, and delivering a series of lectures to a large group of students. In light of this, library schools can serve as agents of change in this arena. Courses in instructional methods would be entirely appropriate as part of such training. These specific skills would be enormously useful to future practitioners as preparation for the responsibilities they will face as academic librarians. Library schools issuing the

Master of Library Science (MLS) degree should offer courses in instructional methods as a major portion of library school curriculum, preparing future practitioners for responsibilities they will face.

For example, the course in BI offered at the University of Washington in Seattle is entitled, Librarianship 600: Bibliographic Instruction. It was initiated in 1982 by Paula Walker, the library instruction coordinator at the University of Washington, and Margaret Chisholm, the director of the Library School at the time. Since 1983, it has been taught and administered by Randy Hensley, an academic librarian in the undergraduate library. Hensley describes the objective of the course as requiring students to explore the theory and practice of BI for the profession in the context of training to deliver BI sessions (Russell & Hensley, 1989).

To attain this goal of practical experience and thorough training in theoretical concepts of BI, the students in the class take part in the Library's program to educate undergraduates in library use. Russell and Hensley (1989) reported that the parts of the course which were most effective in preparing future academic librarians for instruction responsibilities were learning about BI theory and course design, gaining practical teaching experience, observing other instruction librarians, and getting feedback from other librarians.

In 1987, Patterson stated that for many years a large number of academic librarians coming into the profession had neither the educational background nor experience as a teacher. He highlighted the position that it is the responsibility of schools of LIS to prepare academic librarians to adequately teach patrons to use the library so that those individuals can fully utilize library resources. Exposure to this type of instruction should be acquired by the academic librarian while in library school. In the 1960s, several forward-thinking library schools with doctoral programs created such courses as "Seminar in Library Science Teaching" and "Library School Teaching Methods" in an attempt to remedy the situation of academic librarians with no formal preparation or experience in teaching. However, even today, only segments of many courses offered in library schools provide instruction on teaching library user education, and only a handful of schools have an entire course devoted to teaching skills.

In 1993, Shonrock and Mulder discussed the need to examine the standards of library schools and their curriculum as it was vital that academic librarians acquire the skills they need. Instruction demands great attention in the daily work of academic librarians, and training in instructional methodology has always been essential. However, this great emphasis on teaching on the job is not reflected in library school curricula that only rarely include courses focused on pedagogy (Walter, 2008).

Many campuses have been pushing to integrate IL skills since the early 2000s, and academic librarians have been at the center of this discussion. Not only are academic librarians responsible for an increasing amount of instruction, but also for acquisition of the skills for successful delivery of instruction. This can include, but may not be limited to, developing instructional materials with IL competencies in mind, partnering with colleagues yet being prepared to lead, managing classroom dynamics, and assessing student learning. Graduate education in library science must provide academic librarians not only with teaching skills but also the opportunities to hone those skills. Extended teaching practicums that have future librarians working with actual students over time with the guidance of an experienced instructional librarian could provide such an opportunity (Meulemans & Brown, 2001).

Many feel that academic librarians should have the same educational qualifications as academics, be regarded as their teaching peers, and ultimately be granted academic status. Others feel that academic librarians should not have academic status. These important discussions provide an opportunity to discuss the relationship between academics and librarians, and the knowledge and practical teaching skills librarians need to become equal teaching partners (Nimon, 2002).

Although academic librarians have found increased demand to act and think as teachers, few are provided with training in how to teach during their professional education. Studies conducted in the 1970 and 1980s show an almost complete absence of formal course work on instruction. Although still not widely available, formal course work on instruction is gradually becoming a part of the curriculum offered to future academic librarians. However, this is often an irregularly scheduled elective course, or a course required only of certain students, such as those preparing for a career in school libraries (Walter, 2008).

Click and Walker (2009) discussed several studies that were conducted to determine the percentage of LIS programs that regularly offer instructional courses. Westbrook's (1999) study showed that 50% of American Library Association (ALA)-accredited LIS programs offered instruction courses. This increased to 58% in Albrecht and Baron's (2002) study, and rose to 63% when instruction training is a part of another course. However, in their December 2008 study, Click and Walker found that only 40% of respondents had taken a course on library instruction during their professional degree course work. Fifty-three percent of the respondents who did not take an instruction course during graduate school stated that there was no course of this type available. Bewick and Corrall's (2010) study in the United Kingdom (UK) attempted to identify the level of pedagogical knowledge possessed by academic teaching librarians. Results showed that more than half the sample had attended short courses and almost a third had undertaken an extended education or training program to develop their teaching knowledge and skills, but, for the most part, it was less formal, for instance, on the job or through trial and error. Of the 82 respondents, 15 gained formal teaching qualifications from their program, a postgraduate certificate being the most common method. Respondents were asked to state the most valuable things they learned from their education or training in teaching. The responses gathered included comments related to learning styles, delivery techniques, planning for sessions, creating an engaging session, and the importance of feedback and reflection.

Today, when instruction is a primary activity for most academic librarians, many library science programs seem not to recognize that trend (Table 1.1).

Factors which may prevent access to or effectiveness of such training include how often a course is offered; whether the course is online versus face to face; courses that do not include practical teaching

Table 1.1 Instruction Courses Offered in Master of Library Science (MLS) Programs in New York State

MLS Program	Course# & Name	Req'd for School Library Media Specialist (SLMS)	Req'd for All	Format	Frequency	# of Credits
Long Island University	LIS 620: Instructional Design & Leadership	Y	N	Classroom & online		3
Long Island University	LIS 626: Teaching Methodologies for SLMS	Y	N	Classroom		3
Pratt Institute	LIS 673: Library Use Instruction		N	Classroom		3
Pratt Institute	LIS 680: Instructional Technologies	Y	N	Classroom		3
Queens College	LBSCI 764: Instruction Technologies for Info Lit	Y	N	Classroom		3
St. Johns University	LIS 304: Librarian as Teacher	N	N	Classroom	Upon sufficient demand	1
Syracuse University	IST 663: Motivation in Info Lit	Y	N	Classroom		3
Syracuse University	ICT 840: Practicum in Teaching	Y	N	Classroom		1–2
University at Albany	IST 649: Info Lit Instruction: Theory & Techniques	N	N	Classroom	Once a year	3
University at Albany	IST 673 Technology in School Library Media Centers	N	N	Classroom	Once a year	3
University at Buffalo	LIS 523: User Education	N	N	Online only	Once a year	3

Davies-Hoffman, K., Alvarez, B., Costello, M., & Emerson, D. (2013). Keeping pace with information literacy instruction for the real world: when will MLS programs wake up and smell the LILACs? *Communications in Information Literacy, 7*(1), 9–23.

experience; and degree programs that do not require teaching (Davies-Hoffman, Alvarez, Costello, & Emerson, 2013).

Preparation to instruct is vital, simply because it is extremely difficult to help students learn without a basic understanding of the theory and psychology of how students learn. Teaching librarians who lack this sort of preparation will not have a clear understanding of their instruction goals, and are unlikely to be successful instructors. Effective teaching requires an understanding of how students learn and an ability to tailor the instruction accordingly. To adopt this student-centered approach, teaching librarians must be sufficiently prepared with current best practices in educational theory and their application in the classroom (Brecher & Klipfel, 2014).

Some MLS graduates who have completed a course on instruction often comment about the minimal effectiveness and poor quality of the experience. For example, one graduate said, "I took the library instruction class, but, based on this library instruction class, I didn't [sic] walk away with an idea that this was such a big thing because the class was not a very well-done class, it was just sort-of slap-dash thrown together" (Walter, 2008, p. 62).

However, others such as Brecher and Klipfel (2014) felt that even a minimal amount of education course work can be extremely valuable when applying for academic librarian positions. Completing education course work differentiates those candidates from others who may not be able to articulate the rationale behind the structure of library instruction sessions. During job interviews, candidates may be questioned about teaching methods and the philosophies behind them. Exposure to educational literature and practical training can lead to successful conversations about the purpose and value of library instruction. In addition, for new academic librarians the information in education courses can be applied immediately to instructional work with students. Creating lesson plans with current education theory in mind can make library instruction sessions more focused, engaging, and outcome oriented. Pursuing education courses outside of the library school curriculum is a path that some library school students are following. This trend is welcomed by those who feel that MLS students who explore this option will be better prepared not only for their first instruction position, but to become leaders in the area of IL instruction (Brecher & Klipfel, 2014).

The instruction courses investigated by Mbabu (2009) tend to offer traditional training in learning theory, instructional design, teaching techniques, and program management, but mostly focused on developing lower-level IL skills. In more than half of examined courses, Julien & Pecoskie (2009) noted that they often lack coverage of basic IL concepts, outcomes evaluation, needs assessment, or web-based instructional strategies. A shortage of experiential learning and practical application of theory was also observed. According to Pappert (as cited in Davies-Hoffman et al., 2013), students who are unable to take a course combining theory and the practice of teaching lose about half of the information necessary to develop and conduct a comprehensive instruction session.

Hall's (2013) study had many respondents indicating that they believe library school is a good place to start with developing instructional skills, and many believe that library school should do a better job of preparing librarians for instruction. Findings related to formal instruction preparation confirm that those who participated in formal preparation for instruction were more likely to expect teaching to be a part of academic librarianship, feel prepared for this role, as well as see instruction as a major part of their professional life. They were also more likely to participate in continuing education for instructional activities.

In Julien and Genuis (2011) study almost one-third of participants were unsure about or did not expect to have a teaching role when they first began working in libraries. This group of participants was also not likely to have participated in formal preparation for the role of instructor. To solidify instruction as a fundamental part of a librarians' professional role, those who educate librarians for future teaching roles should provide regular, formal instructional opportunities within Master of Library Science (MLS) programs. Perhaps, the sentiments that many librarians share about their preparation to teach can be summed up by this quote,

"Not coming from a teaching background, we were all feeling in the dark in hopes of finding the right approach to teaching" (Donnelly, 2000, p. 49).

1.3 GAINING PRACTICAL TEACHING EXPERIENCE

In the face of this absence of formal teaching preparation, academic librarians have handled this challenge in a variety of ways. One such approach is through on-the-job experience. In 1993, Shonrock and Mulder stated that, although more and more academic librarian positions were required to have practical teaching experience and the ability to provide BI, most librarians did not have the skills needed to effectively provide instruction. Their 1989 study found that academic librarians gained instruction proficiency primarily through on-the-job training, although most librarians felt that formal education was the preferred method of learning skills such as curriculum and instructional design.

Pursuing continuing education is another approach which academic librarians use to make up for the inconsistent availability of formal course work on instruction in MLS programs. Continuing education opportunities range from those provided through professional associations such as the ALA and the Association of College and Research Libraries (ACRL), to workshops and conference programs organized by academic libraries and regional library groups (Shonrock & Mulder, 1993). The ACRL IL Immersion program is mentioned specifically by several respondents and is undoubtedly a tremendous learning experience. In addition to major programs like Immersion and national conferences, librarians should also take advantage of smaller, more local opportunities (Hall, 2013). Along with continuing education, other approaches include in-house orientation, professional development programs, participation in workshops and professional conferences, support of colleagues, role models, or mentors, and consultation with faculty colleagues (Walter, 2008).

Although on-the-job instruction training is available at many academic libraries, Click and Walker's (2009) study found that on-the-job training for instruction was lacking, and many new librarians sought training on their own, not holding their institutions responsible or faulting them for lack of training. Respondent comments revealed that most training was informal, and included observation and coteaching. Most training was conducted through actual teaching. One of the conclusions of the study was that institutions need to find more creative ways for librarians to acquire this type of training. Bewick and Corrall's (2010) study showed that whereas less than half of the respondents had taken short courses or continuing education programs to develop teaching knowledge and skills, most took the less formal approach of learning on-the-job or through trial and error. Other respondent approaches included peer observation or shadowing, reading, research, and even other types of public performance such as acting, music, and public speaking.

Julien and Genuis (2011) survey of librarians found that the majority prepared for instruction through informal on-the-job means, whereas Click and Walker (2010) found many librarians dissatisfied with the availability and quality of on-the-job training. Many indicated that, whereas they desired more training, this became less important as they gained actual classroom teaching experience and got informal feedback from faculty, students, and colleagues. Administrators were also surveyed indicating that workshops, conferences, online courses, and webinars, and reading professional literature were seen as highly supported activities. Administrators also endorsed observation of instruction and feedback from colleagues as the two most successful training activities. They also responded that they considered new librarians needing the most improvement in the areas of preparing lesson plans and public speaking.

Hall (2013) worried about the employer tendency to provide new-hire training through observation and on-the-job training. Although this type of training is a vital aspect of the orientation of a new librarian, a solid background in basic pedagogy would enhance this experience even further. Students who are taught by new academic librarians would benefit more from those who have had the combined training of theory and practice. Hall questions whether on-the-job instruction training is truly one of the best approaches or if it is simply the least costly in terms of dollars.

For many academic librarians, teaching becomes the focus of their professional development activities (Donnelly, 2000). Some view the development of effective teaching skills as an ongoing endeavor, not only through planning and preparation, but by developing a personal instructional style. Akers (2004) suggested that librarians can cultivate an instructional style by teaching as often as possible, observing and learning from colleagues, and keeping the needs of students and faculty in mind.

Walter (2006) felt that it is the responsibility of every teaching librarian to improve their instruction skills as it becomes an increasingly important part of their daily work. Library administrators are also charged with designing effective instructional improvement programs to create a culture of teaching that can ease the transition and support new instructional librarians. Instructional improvement programs may include topics such as basic pedagogy, instructional design, student assessment techniques, how to integrate active learning, and incorporating technology with instruction.

Instructional improvement programs should also provide the opportunity for academic librarians to talk about teaching with their colleagues through peer coaching, evaluation, and assessment of teaching. Peer observation is another way that academic librarians can develop as teachers and provide a better teaching experience for students (Castle, 2009). Also known as peer coaching or coteaching, this approach is an effective way for librarians to strengthen their instructional skills and develop teaching strategies. Coteaching also allows for heightened student engagement and employing of new instructional technologies. Academic librarians inevitably bring together differing skill sets, knowledge, and perspectives for the benefit of students and, in turn, benefit by sharing experiences, insights, and transformative discussions.

Ultimately, the instructor is provided with valuable feedback and different viewpoints, which can result in increased confidence, skill level, motivation, and professional satisfaction (Medaille & Shannon, 2012). Another similar term is the critical-friend method of giving and receiving structured feedback in peer observations. This method may benefit the individual librarian, as well as the organization at large by reflecting upon, improving, and developing teaching skills (Hultman Ozek, Edgren, & Jander, 2012).

As a complement to practical teaching experience, many new academic librarians also take the initiative to familiarize themselves with pedagogical theory. Bladek and Okamoto (2014) describe themselves as recent library school graduates, finding themselves underprepared for the challenge of teaching. Although they put much thought and effort into preparing classes and workshops, they were not always successful. Frustrated with their inability to engage students and discouraged by the results of their student survey, they decided to look for strategies to become better teachers. They looked at the statistical profile of their freshmen and studied the millennial generation. Once they had a better understanding of who their students were, they went on to examine educational theory and research.

Davies-Hoffman et al. (2013) described the Library Instruction Leadership Academy (LILAC) semester-long training program offered in western New York state designed to support education and professional development of librarians combining workshop training along with assigned readings, reflective journaling, and participation. One particular session, Librarian as Educator: From Theory to Practice, presents key trends in educational theory and the implications for library instruction. Participants are asked to consider general principles of learning and brainstorm potential approaches to teaching within the context of IL.

For new academic librarians learning to teach on-the-job, Brecher and Klipfel (2014) offer specific suggestions, such as getting involved in the library and education blogosphere community; participating in nonlibrary continuing education for educators; and browsing general interest education and educational psychology books. Resources such as these are a great introduction to new pedagogy and offer ideas for incorporating them into class sessions.

1.4 CHARACTERISTICS OF TEACHERS VERSUS LIBRARIANS

The word "teacher" is defined as someone who instructs or provides instruction and the verb "to teach" is defined as providing instruction on how to do something. Teaching is also defined as the act of relaying information about a subject. Other terms used to define teaching include to show, present, direct, and guide (Simpson & Weiner, 1998).

Polger and Okamoto (2010) defined a teacher as anyone who uses a variety of methods to share knowledge with another person. This very broad definition leads to the question of what makes a teacher when one considers credentials, skills, professional identity, and regular practice. Historically, teacher education programs have focused on the development of teaching competencies and skills, with little attention directed toward issues of professional identity development. As student teachers develop as professionals it is important to foster the emergence, development, and promotion of the "teacher identity" as an integral part of preservice and continuing professional education. Teacher educators suggest that focus on the development of professional identity is critical to the success of both preservice professional education programs and in-service continuing education opportunities.

From the student perspective teachers are easily identifiable. Children, adolescents, and young adults have greater exposure to the profession of teaching through their experience as students than they do to any other single profession. Students learn what it means to be a teacher through direct observation of education professionals at work. This is not the case with librarians, stereotyped as the bespectacled, middle-aged matron with her premature graying hair coiffed in an austere bun, and shushing young patrons in a library (Walter, 2008).

Berry (2001) observed that most people learn that the totality of the work done by the lady with her hair in a bun involves checking out books and frequently shushing library users. Today the public knows even less about what the modern librarian does. New stereotypes inform us that today's hip, attractive librarians are all good role models, as well as technology wizards. Fialkoff (2007) discussed other professional stereotypes, such as women physicians, who she notes are not mocked for wearing low-heeled comfortable shoes or eyeglasses that hang on chains. She wonders why the stereotypical image of librarian still irritates many librarians in the profession, and points out that some librarians are lightening up and making fun of this image. Many librarians idealize the professional image, assuming that the public sees them in the same way, and are disappointed when this is not the case.

The personality of the librarian has been generally characterized in a negative light, that is, unattractive, rigid, punitive, unfriendly, or at best, timid, shy, and unassuming. In popular depictions librarians are portrayed as introverts. The introvert/extrovert dichotomy was introduced in 1921 by psychologist C.G. Jung, who described introverts as inward-focused and more oriented toward feeling and thought, compared to extroverts who are focused on external people and events (Bartlett, 2012).

Using the Myers–Briggs Type Indicator (MBTI), Williamson (2002) attempted to classify the character traits of librarians in 28 films, such as Evie Carnahan in The Mummy, Marian Paroo in The Music Man, and Bunny Watson in Desk Set. The MBTI provides 16 possible type combinations (Introversion or Extroversion, Sensing or Intuition, Thinking or Feeling, Judging or Perceiving). Most of the librarians were classified as ISFJ, or Introverted-Sensing-Feeling-Judging. According to MBTI, the ISFJ individual can be characterized as: quiet, friendly, responsible, conscientious, thorough, painstaking, and accurate, loyal, considerate, and orderly (Bartlett, 2012).

Furthermore, the way the public perceives the LIS profession was identified as a key factor affecting young people's choice of following the LIS discipline or not. This is particularly significant because perceptions of reality rather than any objective reality are of fundamental importance when making a choice of field of study. There is evidence of discrepancy between the professional roles and the services modern libraries provide and how these are perceived by the public. Misconceptions about librarians' professional responsibilities and duties have persisted over time. The profession is still thought to be female dominated, and is not considered an interesting profession requiring special educational qualifications. Although a number of researchers argued that the image of the profession would improve following the changes in the information field, the public still has a mixed understanding of both libraries and the image of librarians. Nevertheless, the image of the librarian took a long time to develop into what it is today, and may possibly develop into something else over time (Vassilakaki & Moniarou-Papaconstantinou, 2014).

The public, having limited contact with libraries as compared to the classroom, has little comprehension of what a librarian does. Academic librarians suggest that the public views their role as clerical in nature, and that this perception has led to a desire to be recognized as part of an intellectual profession (Walter, 2008). Even within the educational institution, academic librarians are endlessly justifying their professional role (Loesch, 2010). Often referred to as an "accidental profession," librarianship is generally viewed as a field that one pursues while detouring from some other planned career. In the academic environment, librarians can suffer from the lack of a distinct professional identity. In attempts to define themselves as teachers they are often unsuccessful due to major differences between the professional responsibilities of academic librarians and teaching faculty (Walter, 2008).

There are many distinctions between the occupation of librarian and that of academic scholar. On the one hand, academic librarians conduct themselves as members of a "professional" occupation, characterized by formalized training, an established set of credentials, and a code of ethics. There is significant emphasis placed on delivering expert service, as well as the relationship between professional and client. Faculty, on the other hand, operates within a more collegial structure, in which peers rather than clients judge the quality of scholarly work (Fleming-May & Douglass, 2014). Traditionally, the hierarchy of campus culture places research over teaching roles, and also separates scholars from service providers such as librarians (Julien & Pecoskie, 2009). Faculty research, for instance, is mostly considered to be proprietary, and sometimes even competitive as faculty members strive for prestige and tenure. Their research is conducted in a solitary manner, which ensures exclusive control over teaching and research projects, whereas librarianship has a longstanding culture of sharing ideas and processes (Anthony, 2010).

Although academic librarians work full days year round, mainly in the library, which may be separated from other academic buildings on campus, faculty often teach only a few days a week and have summers off to conduct research. Academic librarians often work a somewhat inflexible schedule spanning days, nights, and weekends.

Expectations of faculty, such as preparing lessons, grading exams and papers, and counseling students, along with "unstructured time" for research, writing, and committee meetings, are built into their schedules. Even when librarians are also members of the faculty with requirements for research and publication, they are usually required to work a 40-h week, yet are not relieved of their regular library duties (Anthony, 2010).

Despite these differences, academic librarians must seek out professors with whom to collaborate on IL instruction. However, faculty can be resistant to partnering with librarians in their classroom activities. Also, because faculty outnumber academic librarians on campus, they have a greater presence on academic governing committees. As well, many faculty members feel that librarianship is not a true science and that the MLS provides a vocational rather than an academic education. Not surprisingly, these attitudes serve to reinforce the division in rank between faculty and librarians (Loesch, 2010).

Many faculty members share their students' inability to differentiate between librarians and support staff and the scope of the work that they do. Not many faculty members are aware of the range of instructional duties that academic librarians are responsible for. Although the librarians are aware of faculty responsibilities, faculty often have no real awareness of the work of librarians. Some even fail to understand that the online databases that they use are library materials that must be collected and organized by librarians (Anthony, 2010). They do not consider teaching a significant responsibility for librarians when compared with other responsibilities that they associate with the profession (Walter, 2008). Whereas teachers tend to be concerned with content and its dissemination, academic librarians tend to inform and respond to content. Moreover, whereas faculty members teach credit-bearing, semester-long courses, even today, librarians usually teach single, one-shot library sessions (Polger & Okamoto, 2010).

The culture of academia tends to reinforce social differences between faculty and others on campus. Though some academic librarians have attempted to reinforce their professionalism by gaining faculty status, librarianship is still seen as a service-oriented profession by others and even by librarians themselves. Librarians are often viewed as servers or handmaidens who assist faculty members in their research and instruction. This view of librarians as servers or hand-maidens can imply subordination. Additionally, if faculty members consider librarians inexperienced or lacking the proper credentials in teaching and research, service can be confused with servitude (Anthony, 2010).

The apparent disconnect between academic librarians and faculty can also be created by the different organizational subcultures of governing committees, the organizational structures for behavior, and even the physical layout of the campus. Anthony (2010) observed that the cultures that grow out of these aspects of the academic organization are not necessarily related to issues of social status. Instead, they may be related to who serves on campus committees, the location of faculty offices and classrooms in proximity to the library, and the differences between the roles of faculty member compared to those of the academic librarian. Although faculty members are stationed in different buildings and departments all over the campus, the librarian's base of operations is, of course, the library. These factors can dictate how often the two groups interact or collaborate. Although these attitudes may be changing, and faculty exhibit more and more respect for academic librarians and their work, many still acknowledge that the differences between the two groups have been a part of academic institutions since the beginning, and conclude that these differences are important (Anthony, 2010).

Even when librarians are gaining somewhat of a foothold in classrooms, there is still a great contrast between the language used by academic librarians and faculty members. Albitz and Shelburne (2007) examined faculty and academic librarian conceptions about the concepts of critical thinking and IL. There are some major differences between the two definitions, in that, whereas critical thinking suggests a process, IL suggests a final outcome. The difference between these two basic definitions points to how each group functions in the role of teacher (Anthony, 2010).

1.5 THE TEACHING LIBRARIAN

Despite the apparent differences in how teachers and librarians function in the role of teacher, the job of the academic librarian and the function of the teacher are connected in the most basic way. The teacher's main responsibility is to present information to the student in a systematic and logical way with the goal of increasing the student's knowledge. The daily tasks of the academic librarian are also intended to fulfill this objective. When the patron approaches the academic librarian at the reference desk needing information, his goal is to increase his personal store of knowledge. So the academic librarian, even in the simplest transfer of information at the reference desk, performs the function of teacher (Budd, 1982).

The reference desk can be considered a site for teaching in that the reference interview is primary to the teaching function of reference librarians, and given that the library is an integral part of the academic mission of colleges. The very nature of reference work involves teaching. Academic librarians not only teach users how to use the library, but also assist them in subject area research. Moreover, with many teaching librarians holding secondary Master's degrees with specific-subject expertise, they are able to enhance student learning (Polger & Okamoto, 2010).

The teaching librarian's goal is to impart skills and strategies which will assist students in producing broader, narrower, and related terms for a variety of purposes for use with a myriad of information tools. Actually demonstrating these skills is vital, along with allowing students the time to practice these strategies while navigating through large amounts of electronic text (Branch & Oberg, 2001).

Traditional user education methods such as library orientation, library instruction, and BI have changed because of the development of IL initiatives, which emphasize that the traditional role of the academic librarian instructor or teacher has also changed significantly because of these developments. So today's academic librarians are asked to go beyond the traditional role of acquiring, organizing, disseminating, and preserving information. They are expected to educate users about effective and efficient methods of information retrieval, evaluation, and usage in addition to fulfilling their traditional roles (Wickramanayake, 2014).

Certainly, the teaching librarian is a librarian first, and a teacher or instructor second. Most have no teaching qualifications, and are usually no more highly qualified than the academic teaching staff. However, although the academic instructor also does not usually have teaching qualifications, most are required to have an advanced degree in their specialization. Today's academic librarian is an instructor, study skills advisor, IT trainer, and information skills teacher in one. Characteristically, the teaching librarian lacks a sense of boundary of responsibility, as is often the case in the culture of higher education (Lupton, 2002).

In terms of the instructional role of the library, changes in the academic library environment have resulted in librarians with not only traditional skills in teaching and presentation, but also skills in instructional design and educational technology. Shank and Dewald's (2012) study asked library administrators to rank the importance of skill sets needed to fulfill the library's instructional role in categories such as instructional design, educational technology, presenting, and teaching (Table 1.2).

Within the realm of instructional design, the ability to create learning outcomes and lesson plans ranked the highest. For educational technologies, the ability to use, integrate, and adopt was seen as

Table 1.2 Please Rank in Order (1 Least Important–4 Most Important) the Importance of the Following Knowledge Domains to Future Newly Created and/or Redefined Positions in Your Library

Top number is the count of respondents selecting the option. Bottom % is percent of the total respondents selecting the option	1	2	3	4	Mean
Instructional design skills	124 43%	77 27%	50 17%	35 12%	1.98
Educational technology skills	74 26%	126 44%	55 19%	31 11%	2.25
Presentation skills	34 12%	47 17%	127 45%	72 26%	2.84
Teaching skills	37 12%	32 10%	72 23%	167 54%	3.19

Shank, J.D., & Dewald, N.H. (2011). Academic library administrators' perceptions of four instructional skills. *College & Research Libraries*, 73(1), 77–93.

highly important. The ability to articulate ideas clearly was the top-rated presentation skill, and the ability to facilitate classroom communication was rated as the highest teaching skill. Other skills needed by academic teaching librarians today are strategic planning, interpersonal skills including communication, and an ability to articulate the importance of IL in the curriculum, organizational skills, assessment skills, as well as teaching knowledge and experience. They are also expected to create classroom assignments requiring library-based research, assignments that aid the development of higher-order thinking, IL skills, and competencies (Shane, 2004).

However, even the most thoughtfully designed IL content, delivered with the most dynamic teaching methods, may not ultimately result in successful learning if students' cognitive, emotional, and social characteristics have not been considered. Matteson's (2014) study explored the relationship between representative constructs of students' emotions, cognition, and IL competency. The strongest relationship to IL was observed with the Emotional Intelligence (EI) construct. In both studies, EI significantly predicted IL scores: The more EI a student possessed, the higher his or her IL score. A central component to new thinking in IL is the need to widen the field of vision to consider the whole student, with a view of individual characteristics across a variety of dimensions that enable a student to become information literate. A complete understanding of how students develop and retain IL skills requires an understanding of their cognitive, emotional, and social development. For IL instruction to be the most effective, the dimensions that make up the whole student should be studied and incorporated into instructional methods.

Teaching librarians are also expected to have the ability to think strategically and to assist with identifying program partners within the library and the institution as a whole. They must be familiar with the broader strategic goals of the academic institution, working to fit the library's instruction agenda into this larger context by working alongside the agendas of others on campus. To ensure the success of their marketing and programming efforts, they must keep the viewpoints of faculty and administration in mind. Awareness of these distinct perspectives and values allow teaching librarians to develop targeted approaches to marketing instruction programming that resonate with both faculty and administration (Shane, 2004).

Further complicating the teaching librarian debate is the growth in the number of librarians who teach credit-bearing courses. Teaching credit-bearing courses allows librarians to better understand the needs of students and become more proactive in service delivery compared to the traditional reference desk service model. Teaching a credit-bearing course can be seen an extension of the service and instructional goals of the profession (Polger & Okamoto 2010). It is becoming quite common for academic institutions to expect reference librarians to have classroom teaching experience and even degrees in education.

So it is quite apparent that the teaching librarian has been criticized over the years. One of the biggest criticisms of academic librarians who teach is that it takes them away from their primary role of delivering information. In this view the librarian answers the question rather than teaches the patron how to find the answer for themselves. Schiller (as cited in Lorenzen, 2001) wrote that she questioned the need for anyone in an academic library to be involved in classroom teaching. Schiller believed that academic library instruction took away from the information-providing obligation of the academic library. Later, she would change this view and accept librarians as classroom teachers. In 1981 she wrote that economic and technological developments had made BI and reference services less distinguishable from one another than when she had originally written in 1965. Biggs (as cited in Lorenzen, 2001) felt that academic library instruction took away from the main role of the library, which is to deliver information. She stated that instruction programs would escalate the need for space, materials, and personnel, taking financial resources away from other more important services such as reference. Still others in the profession felt that studies should be conducted to discover if library instruction was worth the money that academic libraries spent on it. Academic library instruction was also criticized as ineffective due to the tendency of many academic librarians to provide much more information than students could ever retain (Lorenzen, 2001).

Shrigley (as cited in Lorenzen, 2001) thought that one-on-one user instruction was more effective than group instruction. Originally in favor of library instruction. He concluded that it was largely a waste of time. Eadie (1990) wrote that gathering students into a classroom and teaching them about the library would fail in educating students. Because students had yet to ask the question that the librarian was teaching them to answer, the student would probably not remember the answer when they eventually need to. Of course, the student would still need assistance later on when they thought to ask the question (usually when the paper was being written) and would then come to the reference desk. Eadie questioned the overall effectiveness of library instruction, and recommended that the money and effort be redirected to references services instead. Wilson (1987) stated that academic librarians in the role of classroom teacher were sort of an organizational fiction. She felt that academic librarians desired greater status in the campus community, which they imagined that faculty had attained due to their teaching role. Librarians then created ways in which they could teach as well, becoming convinced that they were as much teachers as faculty. Wilson argued that few outside of the academic library bought into the ideas that librarians were perpetuating about their teaching, and saw this whole process as counterproductive to the academic librarian.

Of course, many others argue against the criticism that library instruction is ineffective, countering that even if the student still shows up later at the reference desk, the instruction was worthwhile doing. The general argument is that although library instruction will not make students totally independent of librarians, it will increase the number of serious reference questions resulting from student awareness of available resources and librarian expertise. A student will feel more confident in going to and using an academic library if they have had an instruction session with an academic librarian (Lorenzen, 2001).

Despite the many changes and challenges to the role of academic librarian over the last century, it can be said that academic librarians receive greater respect from faculty and administration today. The professionalism and integrity of the library administration and academic librarians have certainly earned them esteem on campus and serve to promote a positive image of the library. A major contributor to this positive image is the ongoing collaboration with faculty in creating effective library instruction sessions for their students. One hundred and thirty-five years after Dewey urged librarians to become educators in 1876; library instruction has become an integrated part of the library structure and, for the teaching librarian, a fundamental responsibility (Zhang, 2001).

REFERENCES

Akers, J. (2004). Discovering your teaching style: seven ways to enhance your classroom presence. *College & Research Libraries News, 65*(5), 251–253.

Albrecht, R. & Baron, S. (2002). The politics of pedagogy: Expectations and reality for information literacy in librarianship. *Journal of Library Administration, 36*(1/2), 71–96.

Albitz, R. S., & Shelburne, W. A. (2007). Marian through the looking glass: the unique evolution of the electronic resources (ER) librarian position. *Collection Management, 32*(1/2), 15–30.

Allen, M. (2008). Promoting critical thinking skills in online information literacy instruction using a constructivist approach. *College & Undergraduate Libraries, 15*(1–2), 21–38. http://dx.doi.org/10.1080/10691310802176780.

Anthony, K. (2010). Reconnecting the disconnects: library outreach to faculty as addressed in the literature. *College & Undergraduate Libraries, 17*(1), 79–92. http://dx.doi.org/10.1080/10691310903584817.

Bartlett, J. A. (2012). New and noteworthy. *Library Leadership & Management, 26*(1), 1–5.

Berry, J. N. (2001). Tell 'em what librarians do each day. *Library Journal, 126*(16), 6.

Bewick, L., & Corrall, S. (2010). Developing librarians as teachers: a study of their pedagogical knowledge. *Journal of Librarianship and Information Science, 42*(2), 97–110.

Bladek, M., & Okamoto, K. (2014). What's theory got to do with it? Applying educational theory and research to revamp freshman library workshops. *College & Undergraduate Libraries, 21*(1), 19–36. http://dx.doi.org/10.1080/10691316.2014.877730.

Branch, J. L., & Oberg, D. (2001). The teacher-librarian in the 21st century: the teacher librarian as instructional leader. *School Libraries in Canada, 21*(2), 9–11.

Brecher, D., & Klipfel, K. M. (2014). Education training for instruction librarians: a shared perspective. *Communications in Information Literacy, 8*(1), 43–49.

Bridges, K. (2001). Why traditional librarianship matters. *American Libraries, 32*(10), 52–54.

Budd, J. (1982). Librarians are teachers. *Library Journal, 107*(18).

Castle, S. (2009). Peer observation and information skills teaching: feel the fear and do it anyway!. *SCONUL Focus,* (45), 72–75.

Click, A., & Walker, C. (2009). Help us help them: Instruction training for LIS students and new librarians. In *LOEX-2009, Albuquerque, NM, April 30–May 2, 2009.*

Click, A., & Walker, C. (2010). Life after library school: on-the-job training for new instruction librarians. *Endnotes, 1*(1), G1–G14.

Creth, S. D. (1995). A changing profession: Central roles for academic librarians. *Advances in Librarianship, 19*, 85–98. http://dx.doi.org/10.1108/S0065-2830(1995)0000019006.

Davies-Hoffman, K., Alvarez, B., Costello, M., & Emerson, D. (2013). Keeping pace with information literacy instruction for the real world: when will MLS programs wake up and smell the LILACs? *Communications in Information Literacy, 7*(1), 9–23.

Donnelly, K. M. (2000). Reflections on what happens when librarians become teachers. *BI at York College of Pennsylvania, 20*(3), 46–49.

Eadie, T. (1990). Immodest proposals: user instruction for students does not work; a former user education librarian challenges a basic belief. *Library Journal, 115*, 42–45.

Ellis, J., & Phillips, A. (2013). Re-defining the service experience: forging collaboration between librarians and students. *Library Management, 34*(8/9), 603–618. http://dx.doi.org/10.1108/LM-10-2012-0070.

Fialkoff, F. (2007). The image thing. *Library Journal, 132*(3), 8.

Fleming-May, R. A., & Douglass, K. (2014). Framing librarianship in the academy: an analysis using Bolman and Deal's model of organizations. *College & Research Libraries, 75*(3), 389–415.

Goetsch, L. A. (2008). Reinventing our work: new and emerging roles for academic librarians. *Journal of Library Administration, 48*(2), 157–172. http://dx.doi.org/10.1080/01930820802231351.

Hall, R. A. (2013). Beyond the job ad: employers and library instruction. *College & Research Libraries, 74*(1), 24–38.

Helfer, D. S. (1997). Not your traditional librarian anymore!. *Searcher: The Magazine for Database Professionals, 5*, 66–67.

Hopkins, F. L. (1982). A century of bibliographic instruction: the historical claim to professional and academic legitimacy. *College & Research Libraries, 43*(3), 192–198.

Hultman Özek, Y., Edgren, G., & Jandér, K. (2012). Implementing the critical friend method for peer feedback among teaching librarians in an academic setting. *Evidence Based Library and Information Practice, 7*(4), 68–81.

Julien, H., & Genuis, S. K. (2011). Librarians' experiences of the teaching role: a national survey of librarians. *Library & Information Science Research, 33*(2), 103–111. http://dx.doi.org/10.1016/j.lisr.2010.09.005.

Julien, H., & Pecoskie, J. (2009). Librarians' experiences of the teaching role: grounded in campus relationships. *Library & Information Science Research, 31*(3), 149–154.

Loesch, M. F. (2010). Librarian as professor: a dynamic new role model. *Education Libraries, 33*(1), 31–37.

Lorenzen, M. (2001). A brief history of library information in the United States of America. *Illinois Libraries, 83*(2), 8–18.

Lupton, M. (2002). The getting of wisdom: reflections of a teaching librarian. *Australian Academic and Research Libraries, 33*(2), 75–85.

Lynch, B. P. (1978). The changing environment of academic libraries. *College & Research Libraries, 39*(1), 10–14.

Matteson, M. L. (2014). The whole student: cognition, emotion, and information literacy. *College & Research Libraries, 75*(6), 862–877. http://dx.doi.org/10.5860/crl.75.6.862.

Mbabu, L. G. (2009). LIS curricula introducing information literacy courses alongside instructional classes. *Journal of Education for Library & Information Science, 50*(3), 203–210.

Medaille, A., & Shannon, A. W. (2012). Co-teaching relationships among librarians and other information professionals. *Collaborative Librarianship, 4*(4), 132–148.

Meulemans, Y. N., & Brown, J. (2001). Educating instruction librarians: a model for library and information science education. *Research Strategies, 18*(4), 253–264. http://dx.doi.org/10.1016/S0734-3310(03)00002-8.

Nimon, M. (2002). Developing lifelong learners: controversy and the educative role of the academic librarian. *Australian Academic and Research Libraries, 33*(1), 14–24.

Ogunsola, L. A. (2011). The next step in librarianship: is the traditional library dead? *Library Philosophy & Practice,* 69–75.

Patterson, C. D. (1987). Librarians as teachers: a component of the educational process. *Journal of Education for Library and Information Science, 28*(1), 3–8. http://dx.doi.org/10.2307/40323630.

Polger, M. A., & Okamoto, K. (2010). "Can't anyone be a teacher anyway?": student perceptions of academic librarians as teachers. *Library Philosophy & Practice*, 1–16.

Russell, T., & Hensley, R. (1989). Education for bibliographic instruction: a recent graduate's view. *Renaissance Quarterly*, *29*(2), 189–192.

Shane, J. M. Y. (2004). Formal and informal structures for collaboration on a campus-wide information literacy program. *Resource Sharing & Information Networks*, *17*(1/2), 85–110.

Shank, J. D., & Dewald, N. H. (2012). Academic library administrators' perceptions of four instructional skills. *College & Research Libraries*, *73*(1), 78–93.

Shen, Z., & Gresham, K. (2000). When technology transforms research methodology: the role of librarians in reforming the curriculum. *Reference Services Review*, *28*(4), 360–368.

Shepley, S. E. (2009). Building a virtual campus: librarians as collaborators in online course development and learning. *Journal of Library Administration*, *49*(1–2), 89–95. http://dx.doi.org/10.1080/01930820802312821.

Shonrock, D., & Mulder, C. (1993). Instruction librarians: acquiring the proficiencies critical to their work. *College & Research Libraries*, *54*(2), 137–149.

Simpson, J. A., & Weiner, E. S. C. (1998). *Oxford English dictionary*. Oxford: Clarendon Press.

Toy, B. J., Krieger, T., Axford, H. W., Wyatt, J. F., Lynch, B. P., Bridegam, W., et al. (1978). The role of the academic librarian: a symposium. *Journal of Academic Librarianship*, *4*(3), 128–138.

Tucker, J. M. (1980). User education in academic libraries: a century in retrospect. *Library Trends*, *29*(1), 9–26.

Vassilakaki, E., & Moniarou-Papaconstantinou, V. (2014). Identifying the prevailing images in library and information science profession: is the landscape changing? *New Library World*, *115*(7/8), 355–375. http://dx.doi.org/10.1108/NLW-03-2014-0029.

Walter, S. (2006). Instructional improvement: building capacity for the professional development of librarians as teachers. *Reference & User Services Quarterly*, *45*(3), 213–218.

Walter, S. (2008). Librarians as teachers: a qualitative inquiry into professional identity. *College & Research Libraries*, *69*(1), 51–71.

Westbrook, L. (1999). Passing the halfway mark: LIS curricula incorporating user education courses. *Journal of Education for Library and Information Studies*, *40*(2), 92–98.

Wickramanayake, L. (2014). An assessment of academic librarians' instructional performance in Sri Lanka. *Reference Services Review*, *42*(2), 364–383. http://dx.doi.org/10.1108/RSR-03-2013-0018.

Williamson, J. (2002). Jungian/Myers-Briggs personality types of librarians in films. *The Reference Librarian*, *37*(78), 47–59.

Wilson, L. A. (1987). Education for bibliographic instruction: combining practice and theory. *Journal of Education for Library and Information Science*, *28*(1), 17–25. http://dx.doi.org/10.2307/40323632.

Zhang, W. (2001). Building partnerships in liberal arts education: library team teaching. *Reference Services Review*, *29*(2), 141–149.

CHAPTER 2

Academic Library Instruction

2.1 THE HISTORY OF LIBRARY INSTRUCTION

The library as an institution may be ancient, but its roots can only be traced as far back as Germany in the 17th century. Evidence of library instruction was found at Harvard College as early as the 1820s (Salony, 1995). However, the history of modern library instruction began in 1876 when Melville Dewey urged librarians to become educators. Dewey urged librarians to reach beyond the library building and its collections to instruct readers on how to select books wisely (Zhang, 2001).

In the late 19th century academic librarians in the United States began teaching in classrooms and inevitably writing about it. In the 1880s, some academic librarians were already lecturing in the classroom. In 1880, Harvard University's Justin Winsor suggested that it was a good idea to introduce bibliographic tools to certain sections of students. Around the same time, the University of Michigan began offering bibliographic instruction (BI). In fact, between 1876 and 1910, 60 universities were offering library research instruction in various formats (Gunselman & Blakesley, 2012).

By this time, the main objective of many librarians was to turn students into real scholars who would be able to educate themselves and do future research without the aid of either a professor or librarian. Many of the librarians in the late 19th century were also professors, teaching in their areas of specialty on a regular basis. So teaching in the classroom was not a new idea for them. However, dedicating an entire class or course to the use of libraries was indeed a new idea (Lorenzen, 2001).

Azariah Root was among several library professionals organizing and presenting bibliographical lectures at that time. Root's career as chief librarian at Oberlin College Library spans the 40-year period from 1887 to 1927. During Root's tenure, he was active in the library

The Fortuitous Teacher
ISBN 978-0-08-100193-6

education movement, as well as in other library-related activities (Rubin, 1977). However, the first course in bibliography for college credit was offered by R.C. Davis at the University of Michigan in the 1880s. Davis described how he had become frustrated with classroom library lectures. He felt that the students were not acquiring the skills in library use that they needed in one or two or even three lectures. His solution was to offer an entire course on library use. Davis' course on bibliography became the model for similar courses at many other universities (Lorenzen, 2001). By 1912 Davis was identified as being more influential than anyone in furthering the BI movement (Tucker, 1980).

By the early 1900s the full extent of instructional activity was evident. The U.S. Bureau of Education's 1912 report described an ALA survey in which 86% of 149 respondents were offering classes designed to help students develop skills in using library resources. Henry Evans' larger survey at that time found that nearly 20.5% of 446 academic institutions offered instruction in library use. Library instruction for users and library education for future librarians developed at the same time. Courses and lectures were sometimes designed in combination to meet the separate needs of each group. In the 1920s, several new library instruction programs emerged to serve the needs of land-grant institutions (Tucker, 1980).

In 1928 the librarian of Swarthmore College expressed criticism of a lack of depth in the library instruction usually given to freshmen and suggested establishing academic departments of bibliography that could offer sequenced courses in library research. In 1934 Louis Shores first described his idea of a library-college in which teaching librarians would collaborate with subject-specialist professors to guide undergraduates in independent, interdisciplinary study. Harvie Branscomb, in a report commissioned by the Association of American Colleges, made a similar recommendation in 1940 (Hopkins, 1982).

Just as in the 1920s, the 1930s was a time when efforts were made to establish instruction programs. However, only a small sector of the US population attended college, and concerns often centered on the economic problems of the time. By the end of the 1930s, the curriculum of many institutions was being questioned and changed. The need for BI was again being emphasized in the literature.

In 1931, a study to determine how much students were using the card catalog showed that students did not actually know how to use the card catalog and other bibliographic aids (Salony, 1995).

Hopkins (1982) noted that academic library instruction was for the most part dormant in the library profession from the late 1930s until the early 1960s. Some librarians were still participating in classroom instruction, but the literature shows little activity on the topic (Lorenzen, 2001). Academic libraries responded, as they had in the 1860s and 1870s, with rapid collection growth and with new techniques of organization and retrieval. Consequently, in the 1960s, just as in the 1880s, there was a severe shortage of trained librarians, despite the gradual upgrading of library schools and that the fifth-year master's degree had become standard. As a result, library schools began offering courses in documentation and computer applications, which led to increased job mobility, improved salaries, and some recognition of librarians as technical experts. In academic libraries, directorships formerly held by nonlibrarian scholars were now more often filled by administrators with technical knowledge.

After World War II, enrollment in colleges and universities rose sharply due to a large number of veterans entering college on the Government Issue (GI) Bill. The egalitarian ideals of the day served to promote the idea of college for everyone, and as college enrollment increased, so did funding. Due to these factors, there was a notable increase in BI activity; however, the development of conceptual elements of instruction did not progress. Many colleges with instruction programs saw larger classes with no increase in staff, which became overwhelming for some librarians. In addition, many librarians did not view library instruction as an important function of the library. In a similar vein, during the 1950s many libraries did not take formal responsibility for providing instruction to graduate students, citing lack of staff time, scheduling issues, and diversity of subject matter as problems in offering instruction. Graduate students needing library instruction were often encouraged by faculty to attend general library seminars (Salony, 1995). Throughout the 1950s library instruction was offered routinely and often remedially, if at all. It was almost completely superseded by developments in technical services, which at the time were seen as more interesting, as well as advantageous for the professionalization of librarianship.

Just as the decline of BI early in the century had been the product of social forces in the professional and academic environments, so was its revival in the 1960s (Hopkins, 1982). The 1960s saw the beginning of a grass roots movement in libraries. Librarians at numerous colleges and universities across the country planned library instruction programs with whatever materials were available to them. The discussion of BI also increased. This movement came about because of changes in higher education such as an expanding and more diverse college population. In addition, larger classes necessitated the use of audiovisual aids and technology. Providing students with library skills was seen as important in that it expanded their research skills beyond the use of textbooks. At this point, librarians were generally better trained and had achieved a higher status, which helped to prepare them for the challenge of providing instruction (Salony, 1995).

Technology and audiovisual materials were an aid to librarians as well. In the 1960s, there was growing experimentation with the use of overhead transparencies, tape recordings, slides, and film, whereas the use of closed-circuit television continued. By the late 1960s computer-assisted library instruction began to appear. For example, the teaching machine, a question-and-answer device using slides flashed pictures on a screen in front of individual students, who were then asked questions about the content. Tools such as these allowed academic librarians to reach more students and better illustrate aspects of their instruction (Salony, 1995).

The term BI is a relatively modern construct and has been a focus of the Library and Information Science field only since the 1990s. Each generation of librarians has redefined the term according to the ideas of that time. The librarian of the 1970s viewed BI simply as library orientation, whereas in the 1980s librarians developed ideas and methods for conducting BI and defining it as a way to teach patrons how to conduct library research themselves. In the 1990s, print-oriented library services shifted to a proliferation of information in various formats, including multimedia (Murdock, 1995).

In the 1980s, academic librarians also became more confident about the significance of their teaching role, and so they focused more on teaching concepts like controlled vocabularies, the flow of information, and the differences in research among various disciplines. The goal was to meet the basic needs of students and at the same time teach skills that they could transfer to new situations, information tools, and environments. In other words, they taught their users to learn how to learn using tools such as exercises and workbooks, which is a part of active learning. They also gave tours, as well as created bibliographies, pathfinders, and guides to using reference tools. Large numbers of academic librarians began pushing to serve as guest lecturers in classes, simply referring to this activity as teaching classes. Eventually they became known as "one-shots," meaning they met with a group of students just once over the course of a semester (Grassian, 2004).

During the 1980s and 1990s, librarians reflected on the meaning and complexity of information literacy (IL); that is, its competencies, how people learn them and how they are taught. The concept continued to evolve over the next 20 years, but during the 1990s librarians struggled to understand and communicate the idea, scope, and boundaries of IL. It was often dismissed as a simple set of skills the learners acquire without instruction. With the introduction of the World Wide Web in 1995, IL grew toward incorporating thinking skills rather than just straightforward computer skills. The scope of the definition grew to include knowing how to use and access information on computers, as well as being able to critically reflect on the nature of information itself (Laverty, 2009).

The Association of College and Research Libraries (ACRL, 1989) standard definition of IL includes the ability to estimate the breadth of information needed, efficiently access that information, effectively evaluate the information and its sources, effectively select and incorporate that information, use it to accomplish a specific goal, and understand the issues surrounding the use of information, as well as ethical and legal considerations. With these standards in mind, during the 1990s, librarians projected that future BI would address the knowledge that users must have to use libraries. This includes eliminating obstacles to the use of libraries, improving library systems and services to minimize what users must learn, and forming alliances with faculty and technology staff to create information systems that will help improve students' critical thinking skills (Rettig, 1995).

By the new millennium, the development of academic library instruction had been impacted dramatically by the emergence of new information technologies over the previous twenty years. The demise of card catalogs and the introduction of online catalogs changed the way that librarians taught. The appearance of electronic versions of reference sources that previously existed only in print was the impetus for changes in how library instruction sessions were conducted. The arrival of the Internet and the World Wide Web required librarians to take the lead in teaching users exactly what the Internet and web are useful and not useful for. Further, the emergence of online distance education required librarians to examine their role as classroom teachers when the classroom is a web page (Lorenzen, 2001).

As computer technology exploded in the 1990s, many librarians found themselves marketing instructional services by arguing that, although students might have excellent computer skills, they often did not know how to choose databases, construct effective searches, or locate and analyze resources. Librarians also promoted instruction sessions by promising professors that they would introduce students to more scholarly resources, moving them beyond the simple Internet search. Even today this is still a valid concern, as the disconnection between faculty expectations and student performance remains a key concern throughout higher education literature (Gunselman & Blakesley, 2012).

In 2004, Grassian wrote that supporters of IL defined it as a brand new, much superior approach to library instruction, in stark contrast to the well-meaning but misguided and extremely limited methods and goals of BI. However, she cautioned librarians to examine whether IL was truly different from what academic libraries had been doing for the last 30 years, during which it was simply referred to as library instruction, library skills, or BI.

Today, there is a growing consensus that IL and its related competencies, such as media and digital literacy, critical thinking ability, ability to engage in lifelong learning, and problem-solving abilities, are
essential for individual and community empowerment, workforce
readiness, and global competitiveness. Advocacy for IL is occurring
on not just local or national levels, but through international collaborations such as the 2005 Alexandria Proclamation. This group of leaders stated that IL is a basic human right which is essential to lifelong
learning, empowers people, and promotes social inclusion of all
nations (Weiner, 2012).

2.2 TYPES OF LIBRARY INSTRUCTION

Many academic librarians today tend to teach exactly how they were
taught, using a traditional lecture style. The traditional lecture model
usually involves a librarian-centered approach with an online database demonstration. Demonstrating the use of online tools is adequate; however, IL takes this step further, requiring students to learn
more than just the technicalities (Noe, 2013). The academic librarian
should also consider the variety of formats, delivery methods, and
teaching methodologies for instruction. McAdoo (2012) discusses six
basic formats for library instruction and the focus for each. BI revolves
around the book, the history of books, tools to access them such as
the library catalog, and also focuses on the use of bibliographies.
Library orientation involves the physical location of items and library
services through tours and scavenger hunts, whereas library instruction creates an awareness of those resources and services, but demonstrates how to find library resources and most effectively use them.
Library instruction often takes the form of a single, general workshop
or one-shot session. Course-integrated instruction is similar, teaching
the use of library resources and services, but meeting the needs of
specific assignments or courses over time. Credit-bearing courses on
topics, such as libraries and information, award college credit for taking these specialized courses, and vary according to departmental
requirements. Most comprehensive of all, IL instruction is collaborative in nature, and is integrated into the entire curriculum. It can be

offered by more than one department and may or may not directly involve librarians.

Library instruction can also be delivered via different platforms. Academic librarians should decide on the platform to be used early on in the development phase of instruction. When deciding which platform to use, instructors should consider which is best suited to them and their prospective audience. The delivery platform can take any of three options: direct, indirect, and hybrid. Direct delivery is a traditional style of instruction in which the students and the instructor inhabit the same space and time. Newer technologies such as ITV makes it possible to be "virtually" present but not necessarily face-to-face. In direct delivery the instructor is always tangibly present in the class session. This platform of delivery is most familiar to students, especially older ones, as well as most instructors. Class activities, such as question-and-answer exercises, happen in real time with direct and immediate responses. This platform builds great rapport between students and instructors due to interaction during every class session. However, it can be an inflexible approach for students because it necessitates their physical presence at the time and location of the class (McAdoo, 2012).

Indirect delivery removes the necessity for the instructor to be physically present with students at the time of instruction. Courses managed through the Internet or intranet of a learning management system like Blackboard or E-College are also not bound by place or time, and so provide greater flexibility. Though classes such as these may at times require a face-to-face session, such as, an orientation or a final examination, this platform can allow students to take a class in any place, at any time, and sometimes to go through the course elements at their own pace. However, students who are used to immediate feedback can become frustrated with the delayed timing of interactions with their instructor. Instructors may have issues with a lack of familiarity with software or hardware, the time and effort needed to develop an online course, and compatibility issues with students' personal computers. In light of this, hybrid delivery has become increasingly common, incorporating elements of both direct and indirect delivery, and possibly providing the advantages of each. However, this means that it shares some of their disadvantages as well, though in practice is usually not as problematic. Because the course structure and delivery style is entirely up to the instructor, emphasis can be placed more on one element than another to find a workable balance, minimizing potential issues. For instance, an instructor may present content through face-to-face lectures but post handouts, class notes, and other materials online for students to access at their own pace (McAdoo, 2012).

When choosing an instruction style, teaching librarians should keep in mind that direct delivery is considered a teacher-centered method most often illustrated by the traditional lecture. Indirect and hybrid styles are considered more learner centered and were developed out of the need for a more active instruction experience for the student (Kaplowitz, 2012).

Just after the new millennium, active learning was being written about and discussed quite frequently, as well as integrated IL and online tutorials. More traditional instruction models and methods were studied and discussed much less, often described as inadequate, ineffectual, and even outdated. Although some attempted to adapt traditional instruction methods to today's new approaches, others recommended they be abandoned completely (Hollister & Coe, 2003). Survey participants in Lorenzen's (2001) study indicated that they strongly preferred the active-learning delivery method for classroom instruction. Overall, academic librarians seemed to prefer an instruction method in which students are more actively engaged in the learning process, with less traditional lecturing and more time spent developing IL skills.

Ten years later, the results of another study suggested that active IL instruction has a direct positive effect on student learning outcomes, resulting in less anxiety and more independent use of online library resources. In addition, students are left with improved perceptions of online library resources and tend to value librarians more highly. The findings of this study suggested that IL instruction practitioners may benefit from focusing on active delivery and minimize the use of passive techniques (Detlor, Booker, Serenko, & Julien, 2012).

Alternatively, some feel that active-learning activities take up valuable time during library instruction sessions. For instance, the nature of one-shot instruction sessions means that content not covered at the time cannot be delayed until another class session. Also, from the student perspective active-learning techniques may be viewed as unnecessary, or students may consider the librarian subordinate to their course instructor and so may be unwilling to participate (Hollister & Coe, 2003).

The power of active learner-centered instruction techniques is well established in IL practice. Web 2.0 and the power of gaming have opened up many other types of possibilities. Many academic librarians today feel that questioning, play, and imagination should be at the center of learning. As a result, scavenger hunts, using software such as SCVNGR, have become popular tools for delivering BI. Godwin (2012) encourages librarians to use these technologies not only as a means of gaining user interest, but also as a way to empower them and to start them on their way to creating their own knowledge.

The learner-centered approach is based on principles resulting from research about how people learn. Learner-centered teaching causes actual changes in the parts of the brain related to learning and memory. Research also tells us that learning does not happen in a vacuum. We learn best by testing out our ideas in a community setting, that is, by collaborating with other learners to verify our ideas. In addition, people tend not to truly learn concepts until they have actively explored them. In other words, they need to be involved in the learning process itself, not by simply listening to a lecture but actively playing a role in the experience. This allows them to connect to the material at hand, thereby determining its relevance to their own lives. When a student takes responsibility for their own learning, as well as that of others in the group, it gives them a voice. They are able to decide how they interact with the material, how their learning will be assessed, which resources will be explored, and the topics they will research. This process improves learning, enhances self-confidence and self-esteem because learners feel a sense of ownership and much more connected to the material (Kaplowitz, 2014).

Hollister and Coe's (2003) survey results suggest that course-integrated IL initiatives are a preferred model for instruction. However, this approach has faced practical, ideological, and systemic obstacles within academic institutions, such as limited access to groups of students and unworkable conditions for providing instructional services. As access to students is limited, so is the provision of library instruction. As a result, an overall tension between teaching librarians and faculty continues to exist and extends to traditional versus newer instruction methods. Hollister and Coe (2003) suggested that, with knowledge, training, and experience, academic librarians can provide instructional services in meaningful ways given the opportunity. Liaison activities and faculty outreach are suggested as ways to move beyond these barriers.

However, the results of the Anderson and May's (2010) study show that all instruction methods are equally effective, and have no impact on how well students retain IL skills. This study was conducted to understand how IL functioned in core undergraduate classes. They sought to clarify students' current IL skills and explore how the method of instruction influences the students' ability to retain and apply information on library research to their academic work in the classroom.

Online instruction is a major part of most IL programs today. Instruction librarians at Hofstra University's Axinn Library have been teaching credit-bearing classes since 2001. Their ultimate goal has been to have library instruction become a part of Hofstra's curriculum for first-year and graduate business students. The goal of the study they conducted was to evaluate the practical aspects of credit-bearing library instruction; it confirmed that a majority of libraries offering credit-bearing classes were using online or hybrid instruction methods (Burke, 2011).

At Wake Forest University, two sections of the library's credit-based class "Accessing Information in the 21st century," or LIB100, were introduced as the universities first online courses. It was offered online because the librarians believed that online education was going to have a major impact on higher education and felt the need to explore this avenue, another way to help their students, faculty, and staff to succeed. The librarians offering the class felt that teaching the class was an extremely rewarding experience, and were able to develop a close relationship with the online students. Likewise, the students reported that they felt very close to the instructor and felt comfortable approaching them for assistance. Course evaluations verified the positive feedback despite certain challenges, such as fitting the course work into their schedules. Some even commented that the course should be required and taught online going forward (Harmon & Messina, 2013, Chapter 1).

In general, the ability to take online courses offers students increased flexibility with their schedules. Many nontraditional students, those who live off campus, go to school part-time, have families, and work full time, would benefit from more courses being offered online. Because libraries have changed a great deal since nontraditional students' last attended college, enrolling in an online IL course can give them the confidence and extra tools to do well in their course work. Online courses can also be viewed as a supportive environment for students to develop these skills at their own pace. One of the major benefits of online IL courses is the ability to reach more students anywhere, at any time. However, there are many issues and common pitfalls with online instruction. Both traditional and nontraditional students often lack the technology skills needed to successfully access and navigate an online course. Although students believe that they have online technology skills, learning management systems are not as intuitive as many of the social network platforms with which they are well acquainted. In many online courses, librarians find that they spend a great deal of time fielding questions about navigating the course system. Very often much more time is spent answering these types of questions as compared to questions related to the session content. Taking an online course requires discipline and a daily commitment to set aside time to log-in to the course, review the content, and complete assignments. Nontraditional students often take online courses because they need a learning experience that is flexible and does not overburden their already busy schedule. However, it can be difficult for them to find the time to access an online course even a few times a week. Similarly, younger traditional students often lack the discipline to access a course daily, much less weekly. Graded attendance is a good way to motivate students to attend online IL sessions (Mery & Newby, 2014).

Another frustrating drawback is the lack of access to software programs used in online courses. Students choose to use free or online programs such as OpenOffice or Google Docs. Often, students cannot open documents and complete assignments. Keeping this in mind, instructors are sometimes forced to upload several versions of the same document. Internet browser issues are another common problem, in addition to general operational and audio issues. Network issues can also occur. Other challenges faced by instructors are an inability to get to know students in a more personal manner. Some instructors find it difficult to replicate online the scenario of helping a student choose and narrow a topic which is easily accomplished in a two-way dialog. When IL first moved online there was a general belief among librarians and administrators that they would simply be transferring face-to-face sessions to an online format. Some believed that after initial development the course would take care of itself because it was all online. Today, we know that this is not the case. Ideally, an online IL course-development plan would include a diverse group of team members with varied skills and expertise. The reality is that in most online IL courses, the librarian may have to undertake several roles, such as instructional designer, subject matter expert, technology specialist, marketer, project manager, and, of course, instructor (Mery & Newby, 2014).

2.3 ACADEMIC LIBRARY INSTRUCTION TODAY

Today's modern academic library has seen a marked increase in the use of technology in electronic communication, web-based and multimedia resources, electronic services, and research tools for patrons. The increase in technology use has meant changes in the structure of service and instruction, especially with the online student. In fact, meeting the needs of online students for access, reference, and instruction has led to the greatest technology transformation. It has also lead to the introduction of new and innovative ways of providing IL at a distance through the creation of tutorials and other web-based resources and services. New standards for service have emerged in response to the changing scholarship and scholarly communication patterns brought about by advanced technologies. Other than web-based service, librarians continue to provide instruction in person, by telephone, and through e-mail. Today's multifaceted library instruction reflects not only students' rapidly changing learning styles but also the broad range of faculty expectations and preferences. Instruction methods will vary from traditional lecture style to hands-on, librarian-led workshops. Contemporary instruction methods may include course- and assignment-specific online guides or subject-specific guides. Instruction may also be targeted at faculty, covering library services and electronic resources in a particular subject area (Moyo, 2004).

A common problem among academic libraries today is the minimal use of electronic resources provided by the library. This can be due to a number of factors, such as patrons being unaware that a certain source exists or because they are ill-equipped with the skills to use it. In these situations libraries may benefit from focusing marketing efforts on their virtual academic community, who has the greatest need for electronic resources. Once the virtual community is more aware of available electronic resources, providing IL that is tailored to their specific needs will help to retain their attention. As well, libraries should provide the necessary instruction to equip all patrons with the skills and competencies to make effective use of library resources (Moyo, 2004).

Not only has the amount of library instruction increased in academic libraries, but also the type of information being sought. For example, today's students need to locate and use images in their course work more than ever before. The contemporary information age is as dependent on the image as on the written word. Students may need images for PowerPoint presentations, research essays, or in the design of web pages. Academic librarians have the opportunity to assist students in the development of visual literacy and at the same time engender student enthusiasm for nontraditional texts (Harris, 2007).

Today's academic librarians are tailoring library instruction according to specific courses and assignments. For example, the Information Literacy Education (ILE) project at Washington State University Library is a flexible online learning environment which delivers IL instruction targeted to the needs of specific research assignments. Academic librarians collaborate with course instructors to directly address the IL skills needed to complete an existing research project. Although many institutions have developed comprehensive IL tutorials to provide online instruction, ILE is different in that it pairs the best available web tutorials with the appropriate IL concepts to the specific components of a particular assignment. Expanding the scope of tutorials offered to those available on the web provides much more than any individual tutorial or single institution ever could. In this way, Washington State University Libraries are able to more fully meet the IL instruction needs of their substantial student body (Borrelli, Johnson, & Cummings, 2009). Not only are libraries coming up with creative ways to provide IL instruction, but they are also thinking about ways to save the time of the user. Because of the modern dependence on computers, users tend to believe that librarians should be able to help them save time, leading to high expectations during not only reference interactions but also during IL instruction (Holt, 2010).

Academic librarians are under pressure from various entities to incorporate assessment into their practice of library instruction: assessment of student learning and literacy, of the instruction itself, and of the instruction program. Many of the pressures are altruistic, such as faculty and administrators concerned with improving the IL of today's students, and librarians themselves seeking to improve the quality of the instruction provided. However, other pressures may be financial; for example, many libraries are working to better incorporate IL into standards of higher education yet are unable to hire additional personnel. In Sobel and Sugimoto's (2012) study the majority of respondents conducted assessment, but far fewer than might be expected given the increasing demand for assessment. Even those who did assess student learning spent a small percentage of their time doing so; the majority spent 10% or less of their time. The most popular tool for assessment was worksheet exercises, followed by quizzes given at the end of the session. Most instructors clearly use multiple tools for the assessment of learning. Most respondents learned how to conduct assessment on their own. Fewer than 20% learned how to perform assessment in their Master of Library Science (MLS) program. A third of respondents had never received formal training in statistics. Of those who had, the majority of them learned statistics during their bachelor's degree curriculum (Sobel & Sugimoto, 2012).

Many instruction librarians are taking advantage of opportunities to collaborate directly with student-led organizations. These partnerships have the potential to increase student attendance at library events and provide platforms for students to engage in richer forms of exploratory learning that incorporate 21st century skills. In terms of IL instruction, these collaborative relationships must include learner–librarian, learner–content, and learner–learner interactions. Instruction librarians have the opportunity to reach learners at the highest levels, going beyond the recall and the understanding of content into the higher-level skills of evaluating information and creating new products. Librarians must possess collaboration and communication skills to remain relevant in the 21st century. To augment library instruction, a wide range of collaborative relationships should be developed between the librarian and the student, faculty, subject specialist, and, if possible, the department (Johnson, Clapp, Ewing, & Buhler, 2011). At the department level, librarians can collaborate to design and implement curriculum-integrated, outcomes-assessed library instruction in undergraduate writing-intensive courses (Stowe, 2011).

With the rapid growth of library instruction services comes the need for additional instructional space. Space planning is an important part of a library's existence and growth, making it necessary to evaluate key operations and develop space-planning projects that support the delivery of library resources and services (Wang, 2007).

For most teaching librarians the instruction they provide each semester involves one-shot sessions, usually 1 h per session. During a one-shot session, they will usually provide learner-centered and active-learning opportunities for the students. One way to maximize these activities in short sessions is by using the technique called the flipped classroom. A flipped classroom allows the librarian to create a preinstruction session assignment along with videos or other media, which students will use prior to the session, allowing more classroom time for active learning with the students. This model also provides librarians the opportunity to collaborate with faculty to develop library instruction sessions with preinstruction session assignments and other materials. This model allows for greater collaboration and creation of more engaging library instruction sessions incorporating different types of media, both online and in the classroom. It also creates other collaborative opportunities such as peer teaching. Teaching librarians using this model have a variety of choices when it comes to creating the materials students will use prior to coming to class (Fulkerson, 2014).

Some teaching librarians have compared today's IL instruction to stage performance. For instance, just as in most stage performances they have a limited amount of time to deliver a certain amount of information to their audience. Although professors have a 12-week semester, teaching librarians often have only 60 min and a lot of information to cover. During an instruction session, librarians may find themselves acting as playwright, director, performer, and even stage crew. The student, just like an audience member at a theater performance, has just one opportunity to take in all of the information being delivered at that time. After all, not many people go to see a stage performance more than once. Another aspect that library instruction and stage performance share is repetition. Repetition is a factor for any teacher, but especially for library instructors conducting many one-shot sessions over the course of a single semester. Many of the same elements (such as catalog searching, evaluating sources, or accessing databases remotely) must be covered for each session. Those who work in the world of theater would agree that this is one of the main aspects of theatrical performance (Furay, 2014).

Librarians are not only comparing instruction to stage performance but also looking at how other visual media such as film can be used to deliver IL concepts more effectively. Tewell's 2014 study sought to provide insight into whether televisual media has the capacity to illustrate IL concepts in action. Not only does television introduce the theme for the instruction session, but it is also an interesting medium. This makes it an appealing format for considering the significance of IL in settings beyond the library or campus, such as in distance classes. There are a number of potential benefits to using film to increase student awareness of IL. Visual media, specifically television comedies, can connect students, invoke emotional learning, and act as a framework for communicating challenging concepts (Tewell, 2014).

Based on pre- and posttest findings and focus group sessions in Tewell's (2014) study student learning of selected IL concepts may have improved overall, and, if so, it increased more significantly among students in the experimental group that viewed excerpts from television comedies corresponding to the material being discussed. The results support the author's hypothesis that student learning in regard to selected IL concepts among the experimental group will be higher than that of a control group that participates in only group discussion.

Along with media, the use of games in IL has become quite popular since the start of the new millennium. This trend has developed partly because games help students better understand how to interact with information for problem solving and discovery-based learning when conducting library research. The benefit for students in using games is in the simplification of library jargon and developing familiarity with library resources. Librarians benefit from the use of games in that they offer another way for students to communicate with them, one of the main objectives of providing IL instruction. Examples of games used in IL sessions (variations on popular games) are Jeopardy, World of Warcraft, and Clue. Overall, games have the capacity to teach people a wide variety of abilities including critical thinking, problem solving, and discovery-based learning. These abilities are connected to the learning outcomes instruction librarians address with students through IL instruction (Porter, 2012).

Rush (2014) describes creating a game based on the board game Candy Land to teach undergraduates about information ethics. The game was based on Candy Land due to its simple structure and for the nostalgia factor (the author informally asked several students what board games they remembered and liked the best from their childhood, and Candy Land was one of the most common answers). The rule sheet was modified, renaming the various aspects and characters in the game to relate them to information ethics and the learning outcomes of the session.

Another related trend in higher education, the use of mobile learning and gaming, has influenced librarians to experiment with a tool called SCVNGR as a way to connect students to the library. SCVNGR is a versatile software application that can be used on a laptop, cellular phone, smartphone, and a variety of other mobile devices. One great reason to use geolocation-based instruction or gaming in libraries is that the building interiors are usually arranged according to function, which lends itself to place-based tours. Materials of all types are shelved in specific places, and there are various offices, departments, and service points that students need to know about. This game lends itself to explaining library policies regarding things such as printing, fines, or food policies. IL can be taught through a gaming platform such as SCVNGR. By using the geolocation component on the mobile device or by texting a pass phrase to a number, teaching librarians are able to engage students with a preset group of question and answers about a location (Vecchione & Mellinger, 2012).

Incorporating gaming and active-learning elements into library instruction can be a very effective way to engage students and increase their knowledge retention. The often fast-paced nature of games speaks to the learning styles of Millennials and encourages active participation by including social elements, a competitive element, and being naturally student centered. Games can be simple and easily incorporated into instruction. Simple nondigital games can be beneficial in two ways. First, they are easy to create, require little technology training, extra funding, or resources. Second, they can be easily adapted and modified as information and instructional needs change (Rush, 2014).

Today's literature also indicates a departure from the so-called "traditional models" of providing library instruction, such as the

1-h/one-shot class, and the lecture and demonstration method of teaching. On the other hand, in Hollister and Coe's (2003) study instruction librarians were surveyed regarding their views on current trends versus traditional models of library instruction. Results of the survey suggest that traditional methods of instruction continue to be useful, effective, and necessary, especially when merged with today's new, multifaceted, and integrated IL initiatives. Overall, respondents to the survey viewed online tutorials as effective instructional tools, though many suspect that there is no significant difference in students' learning outcomes when comparing online instructional methods with lecture and demonstration. Survey respondents were generally opposed to the notion that traditional methods of library instruction, such as the one-shot session, are obsolete.

2.4 ONE-SHOT LIBRARY INSTRUCTION: HOW IS IT UNIQUE?

Today, many of the classes taught by librarians are still single, one-shot sessions. Repetition of content has helped librarians to hone these lecture and demonstration sessions so that they are able to cover essential skills in 50 min or less (Finley, Skarl, Cox, & VanderPol, 2005). The ultimate goal for a one-shot session is to have students actively engage with the librarian and library resources to provide an introduction to the many ways the library supports student learning (Kenney, 2008). One-shot sessions can vary according to session length and the amount of input a librarian has with regard to the course content. This can make it difficult for librarians to meaningfully adapt lesson plans, activities, and assessment tools for their own needs (Bryan & Karshmer, 2013). One-shot sessions are usually either 50- or 80-min long and tend to be focused on a specific research project. The vast majority of these sessions are hands-on and take place in computer labs (Willson, 2012), during general orientation sessions or within credit-course class time (Hanz & Lange, 2013).

Some librarians feel that one-shot workshops and orientations typically cover too much information and too often rely on passive learning (Houlson, 2007). Despite this, one-shot sessions are still the most common mode of instruction (Phelps, Senior, & Diller, 2011). Houlihan and Click's (2012) study showed that the demand for one-shot sessions increased noticeably for the 2010–11 academic year— from 43 in 2009–10 to 101 for Fall 2010 and Spring 2011. Thirty respondents teach the traditional "one-shot" or one-time, in-person course-integrated session (94%); online one-time course-integrated sessions (36.36%) studies have documented the continued prevalence of one-shot sessions and fewer credit courses. One-shot library sessions frequently depend on individual faculty's willingness to give up class time, or even to recognize IL as a worthy goal (Phelps et al., 2011).

In fact, many faculty and teaching assistants prefer the traditional one-shot model of library instruction, in which the librarian is invited to present during one class session on the effective use of library resources. Some instructors use the one-shot session for large 200-plus student lectures, whereas others prefer to use it for a class size of 20 to 24 students. For the latter, sessions are conducted in networked computer classrooms, in which students are able to get valuable hands-on experience using electronic library resources. Given the popularity of this type of instruction, it appears that instruction librarians still believe in its usefulness, effectiveness, and necessity in the classroom (Hollister, 2008). One-shot sessions appear to be a mainstay in most library instruction programs. Instruction librarians are given a single class session to teach students how to conduct library research. A lot of information is usually covered in a short period of time (Mahaffy, 2012). Academic librarians today conduct more one-shot instruction (either generic or subject-specific) than any other kind. It also serves the purpose of simply introducing students to the library and familiarizing them with research tools. However, some feel that one-shot instruction is not IL, but a familiarization exercise that provides a gateway to IL (Badke, 2009).

Many librarians are making excellent progress toward embedded library instruction, however due to the prevalence of the traditional one-shot instruction session, their structure and objectives must be addressed. Determining what to teach in a one-shot library instruction session for a freshman writing class can be formidable. Traditional "library orientation" sessions can focus anywhere from the library building itself, to the website, the online public access catalog, or other basic concepts. The academic librarian's goal is to teach the students enough to prepare them for college-level research, but time limitations can make this a difficult task to accomplish (Swoger, 2011).

Many colleges and universities have moved beyond one-shot sessions to integrate IL into their curricula at the program and institutional level (Saunders, 2012). Although there are possibly more effective methods of teaching IL (eg, embedded librarians, credit-bearing courses) the familiar one-shot session is the model that many academic librarians are being required to work with (Spievak & Hayes-Bohanan, 2013). Considering this situation, a 50-min one-shot session has questionable impact on students' IL skills. With these time limitations in mind, most librarians develop online tutorials to supplement the process of learning specific information skills, to more fully address student needs (Domínguez-Flores & Wang, 2011).

The typical "one-shot" session involves a class full of freshman students whose instructor marches them dutifully to the library. Here, a librarian presents them with an introductory lesson that attempts to cram as much information about as many library resources as possible into a single class period, usually 50 min or less. Many studies have criticized this instruction model, including Badke (2009), who, although he believes the one-shot can be beneficial as a hands-on introductory tool, insists that "we need to stop believing that anyone becomes information literate (even somewhat so) in an hour. It does not happen" (p. 42). Jacobs and Jacobs's (2009) study further discussed the erroneous notion that "a single 'dose' of library instruction" provides sufficient knowledge of the complexities of college-level research. The one-shot lacks the necessary time to assess student's individual research needs, skill levels, and learning styles. Students regard the librarian as a "guest lecturer" rather than a coteacher and tend to tune out. In general, librarians have struggled to make one-shot instruction productive due to the noncredit nature of the course and the lack of specific research assignments to which instruction might be tailored (Bean & Thomas, 2010).

Teaching comprehensive IL skills is almost impossible when time is limited. It is understood that students need more IL instruction than can be offered in a one-shot class (Gustavson, Whitehurst, & Hisle, 2011). It is unrealistic to expect students to become information literate in just one class session. One-shot IL sessions, although they may be effective in some ways, should be only one part of an overall library instruction program. Complex IL instruction cannot take place in a one-shot session as these skills are complex and take time to develop (Willson, 2012).

One of the pitfalls of one-shot instruction is the common "drill and kill" method of lecture and practice through rote repetition (Little, 2012). However, the structure of one-shot sessions should be reconsidered to avoid too much lecture and demonstration, which can further hinder learning. Instructors might also consider addressing the problem of time constraints by including less content but more group work so that students can learn from and teach each other (Houlihan & Click, 2012).

Time constraints make it difficult to conduct extensive evaluations in any library instruction session, but especially so for librarians teaching one-shot sessions. Librarians attempting to assess students in one-shot sessions face challenges, primarily because limited time and contact with the students forces them to focus all of their time and effort on the "delivery" portion of the session (Hanz & Lange, 2013). One-shot sessions can make evaluation extremely tricky. Any effort to measure the impact of such a brief interaction with students is bound to be a challenge, with most one-shot sessions being anywhere from 50 to 80 min in length and encompassing a wide variety of library instruction, from information tools to search techniques (Wang, 2007). One way to counteract this is to use supplemental materials, such as online videos and guides to replace some of the lecture and handouts typical to these types of session. Supplemental materials can also provide additional information for students in one-shot sessions (Hahn, 2011). In addition, restructuring sessions to a more interactive style takes up valuable time but using technology such as clickers and polling can spice up one-shot, increase student engagement, and test prior knowledge (Zdravkovska, Cech, Beygo, & Kackley, 2010).

For those librarians who have the luxury of meeting with students more than once a semester, they can choose to limit the number of outcomes to one or two per session, allowing a more comprehensive focus on specific skills than would most likely be covered in a one-shot session (Carter, 2013). However the true one-shot session, by its nature, cannot provide students with more than an introduction to basic library skills. IL competencies take more time and practice than can be learned in a 50 min class session. Yet Mery, Newby, and Peng's (2012) study showed that students who attended a one-shot librarian-taught session did show some significant gains. Results of the study indicate that the one-shot session was helpful in delivering some IL skills and strategies, but it was not consistently effective. These sessions focused on database searching and retrieval of articles, and these are the areas in which students showed the most improvement. However, students did not make significant gains in other skill areas.

It is important for instruction librarians to remember that, more than likely, the session they are planning is not the last time students will be exposed to the library and IL. Because it can feel that way, a librarian may attempt to teach everything in a single session. This amounts to not making any choices about what to teach and can be just as damaging as making the wrong choice about what to teach. In the context of the one-shot session the librarian cannot know the preferences of the individual student and also cannot incorporate all learning styles (Oakleaf et al., 2012). In a semester-long class, an instructor will gain knowledge about his or her students and adapt lesson plans and approaches to fit the class needs. For librarians teaching a one-shot session, this is not an option (Brooks, 2013). Although librarians may think they know what students want and need from a one-shot session, they really cannot know unless they ask them. A quick needs assessment at the beginning of a one-shot class allows librarians to rely on evidence and not simply gut instinct (Oakleaf et al., 2012).

Indeed there is what has been described as a conflict between short-term objectives, that is, the class assignment that produced the instruction session to begin with, and long-term goals such as preparing students for IL and self-directed lifelong learning. Librarians must meet faculty wishes and expectations for the instruction session and at the same time avoid this problem with the one-shot lecture. One consequence of this is that librarians often have a "love/hate relationship with the one-shot session, [which is] both the bread-and-butter and the bane of library instruction" (Nuttall, 2012).

Despite the challenges presented with one-shot instruction, librarians can view them as opportunities. Three instructional challenges on which to concentrate are the importance of preparation, the necessity of effective one-shot performance, and the role of repetition. These three challenges are aspects of teaching that strongly parallel the world of performance. The dominant issue for instruction librarians may be to find the time to incorporate performance techniques such as storytelling in a one-shot instruction session. The use of visuals in library instruction has become increasingly prevalent simply because much of what librarians are trying to teach is essentially visual. Showing versus telling becomes imperative, especially during a one-shot session while teaching students how to access the library catalog, subscription databases, and possibly even physical areas of the library. Many find that the use of humor, another performance technique, is becoming more and more applicable to their work. Librarians can gain invaluable performance advice by attending a stand-up comedy workshop, which shows how to use personal anecdotes, poke fun at oneself, and incorporate pop-culture or other irreverent search examples. Also adding humorous props, images, or even costumes provides a measure of levity to the classroom environment. Many have compared the performance aspect of library instruction sessions to stand-up comedy routines, which must be performed many times over and always to a new audience. Considering this aspect of library instruction may help librarians to find ways to cope with the repetition inherent in library instruction (Furay, 2014).

Clearly, instruction librarians are well aware that the one-shot instruction session is not ideal for true, meaningful transfer or retention of basic research skills, yet continue to strive to impart them. These one-time presentations, which are usually developed to meet the needs of first-year composition or other introductory-level courses, are expected to both acquaint students with library services, as well as teach them how to conduct library research. This includes everything from searching the library catalog to using various databases, and being able to distinguish between the various types and quality of sources. Not surprisingly, these types of instruction sessions can easily overwhelm students with their jam-packed, whirlwind dispersal of information, and can frustrate and overburden the librarians tasked with teaching them (Watson et al., 2013). However, preparing for and incorporating various interactive techniques and elements of performance can provide a solid platform for a successful one-shot instruction session.

REFERENCES

Anderson, K., & May, F. A. (2010). Does the method of instruction matter? An experimental examination of information literacy instruction in the online, blended, and face-to-face classrooms. *The Journal of Academic Librarianship*, *36*(6), 495–500. http://dx.doi.org/10.1016/j.acalib.2010.08.005.

Association of Colleges and Research Libraries. (1989). *Presidential committee on information literacy: Final report.* Retrieved from: http://www.ala.org/acrl//publications/whitepapers/presidential.

Badke, W. (2009). Ramping up the one-shot. *Online*, *33*(2), 47–49.

Bean, T. M., & Thomas, S. N. (2010). Being like both: library instruction methods that outshine the one-shot. *Public Services Quarterly*, *6*(2–3), 237–249. http://dx.doi.org/10.1080/15228959.2010.497746.

Borrelli, S., Johnson, C. M., & Cummings, L. A. (2009). The ILE project: a scalable option for customized information literacy instruction and assessment. *Communications in Information Literacy*, *3*(2), 128–141.

Brooks, A. (2013). Maximizing one-shot impact: using pre-test responses in the information literacy classroom. *Southeastern Librarian*, *61*(1), 41–43.

Bryan, J. E., & Karshmer, E. (2013). Assessment in the one-shot session: using pre- and post-tests to measure innovative instructional strategies among first-year students. *College & Research Libraries*, *74*(6), 574–586.

Burke, M. (2011). Academic libraries and the credit-bearing class: a practical approach. *Communications in Information Literacy*, *5*(2), 156–173.

Carter, T. M. (2013). Use what you have: authentic assessment of in-class activities. *Reference Services Review*, *41*(1), 49–61. http://dx.doi.org/10.1108/00907321311300875.

Detlor, B., Booker, L., Serenko, A., & Julien, H. (2012). Student perceptions of information literacy instruction: the importance of active learning. *Education for Information*, *29*(2), 147–161.

Domínguez-Flores, N., & Wang, L. (2011). Online learning communities: enhancing undergraduate students' acquisition of information skills. *The Journal of Academic Librarianship*, *37*(6), 495–503. http://dx.doi.org/10.1016/j.acalib.2011.07.006.

Finley, P., Skarl, S., Cox, J., & VanderPol, D. (2005). Enhancing library instruction with peer planning. *Reference Services Review*, *33*(1), 112–122. http://dx.doi.org/10.1108/00907320510581423.

Fulkerson, D. (2014). The flipped classroom and media for library instruction: changing library instruction. *Against the Grain*, *26*(4), 17–21.

Furay, J. (2014). Stages of instruction: theatre, pedagogy and information literacy. *Reference Services Review, 42*(2), 209–228. http://dx.doi.org/10.1108/RSR-09-2013-0047.

Godwin, P. (2012). *Information literacy beyond library 2.0.* London, England: Facet Pub.

Grassian, E. (2004). Building on bibliographic instruction. *American Libraries, 35*(9), 51–53.

Gunselman, C., & Blakesley, E. (2012). Enduring visions of instruction in academic libraries: a review of a spirited early twentieth-century discussion. *Portal: Libraries and the Academy, 12*(3), 259–281.

Gustavson, A., Whitehurst, A., & Hisle, D. (2011). Laying the information literacy foundation: a multiple-media solution. *Library Hi Tech, 29*(4), 725–740. http://dx.doi.org/10.1108/07378831111189796.

Hahn, E. (2011). Video lectures help enhance online information literacy course. *Reference Services Review, 40*(1), 49–60. http://dx.doi.org/10.1108/00907321211203621.

Hanz, K., & Lange, J. (2013). Using student questions to direct information literacy workshops. *Reference Services Review, 41*(3), 532–546. http://dx.doi.org/10.1108/RSR-03-2013-0016.

Harmon, C., & Messina, M. (2013). *E-learning in libraries: Best practices.* Lanham: The Scarecrow Press, Inc.

Harris, B. R. (2007). Image-inclusive instruction. *College and Undergraduate Libraries, 14*(2), 65–75. http://dx.doi.org/10.1300/J106v14n02_05.

Hollister, C. V. (2008). Meeting them where they are: library instruction for today's students in the world civilizations course. *Public Services Quarterly, 4*(1), 15–27.

Hollister, C. V., & Coe, J. (2003). Current trends vs. traditional models: librarians' views on the methods of library instruction. *College & Undergraduate Libraries, 10*(2), 49–63. http://dx.doi.org/10.1300/J106v10n02_05.

Holt, G. (2010). Saving time: Ranganathan and the librarian as teacher. *Public Library Quarterly, 29*(1), 64–77.

Hopkins, F. L. (1982). A century of bibliographic instruction: the historical claim to professional and academic legitimacy. *College & Research Libraries, 43*(3), 192–198.

Houlihan, M., & Click, A. (2012). Teaching literacy: methods for studying and improving library instruction. *Evidence Based Library & Information Practice, 7*(4), 35–51.

Houlson, V. (2007). Getting results from one-shot instruction. *College & Undergraduate Libraries, 14*(1), 89–108. http://dx.doi.org/10.1300/J106v14n01_07.

Jacobs, D., & Jacobs, H. L. M. (2009). Transforming the one-shot library session into pedagogical collaboration: information literacy and the English composition class. *Reference & User Services Quarterly, 49,* 72–82.

Johnson, M., Clapp, M. J., Ewing, S. R., & Buhler, A. (2011). Building a participatory culture: collaborating with student organizations for twenty-first century library instruction. *Collaborative Librarianship, 3*(1), 2–15.

Kaplowitz, J. R. (2012). *Transforming information literacy instruction using learner-centered teaching.* New York, NY: Neal-Schuman Publishers, Inc.

Kaplowitz, J. R. (2014). *Designing information literacy instruction: The teaching tripod approach.* Lanham, MD: Rowman & Littlefield.

Kenney, B. F. (2008). Revitalizing the one-shot instruction session using problem-based learning. *Reference & User Services Quarterly, 47*(4), 386–391.

Laverty, C. (2009). Our information literacy heritage: from evolution to revolution. *Feliciter, 55*(3), 88–91.

Little, G. (2012). Teaching with technology: library instruction in a digital context. *The Journal of Academic Librarianship, 38*(4), 242–243. http://dx.doi.org/10.1016/j.acalib.2012.05.001.

Lorenzen, M. (2001). A brief history of library information in the United States of America. *Illinois Libraries, 83*(2), 8–18.

Mahaffy, M. (2012). Student use of library research guides following library instruction. *Communications in Information Literacy, 6*(2), 202–213.

McAdoo, M. L. (2012). *Fundamentals of library instruction*. Chicago, IL: American Library Association.

Mery, Y., & Newby, J. (2014). *Online by design: The essentials of creating information literacy courses*. Lanham: Rowman & Littlefield.

Mery, Y., Newby, J., & Peng, K. K. (2012). Why one-shot information literacy sessions are not the future of instruction: a case for online credit courses. *College & Research Libraries*, *73*(4), 366–377.

Moyo, L. M. (2004). The virtual patron. *Science & Technology Libraries*, *25*(1/2), 185–209.

Murdock, J. (1995). Re-engineering bibliographic instruction: the real task of information literacy. *American Society for Information Science. Bulletin of the American Society for Information Science*, *21*(3), 26–27.

Noe, N. (2013). *Creating and maintaining an information literacy instruction program in the twenty-first century*. Retrieved from: http://www.myilibrary.com.

Nuttall, H. D. (2012). Da Vinci's vitruvian man and the academic instruction librarian: striving for balance. *Mississippi Libraries*, *75*(1), 9–12.

Oakleaf, M., Hoover, S., Woodard, B., Corbin, J., Hensley, R., Wakimoto, D., et al. (2012). Notes from the field. *Communications in Information Literacy*, *6*(1), 5–23.

Phelps, S. F., Senior, H. E. K., & Diller, K. R. (2011). Learning from each other: a report on information literacy programs at Orbis Cascade Alliance libraries. *Collaborative Librarianship*, *3*(3), 140–153.

Porter, T. D. (2012). Games and activities: an alternative foundation for library instructional learning. *Codex*, *2*(2), 61–77.

Rettig, J. (1995). The convergence of the twain or titanic collision? Bi and reference in the 1990s' sea of change. *Reference Services Review*, *23*(1), 7–20. http://dx.doi.org/10.1108/eb049233.

Rubin, R. (1977). Azariah Smith Root and library instruction at Oberlin College. *Journal of Library History*, *12*(3), 250–261.

Rush, L. (2014). Learning through play, the old school way: teaching information ethics to millennials. *Journal of Library Innovation*, *5*(2), 1–14.

Salony, M. F. (1995). The history of bibliographic instruction: changing trends from books to the electronic world. *Reference Librarian*, *24*(51/52), 31–51.

Saunders, L. (2012). Faculty perspectives on information literacy as a student learning outcome. *Journal of Academic Librarianship*, *38*(4), 226–236. http://dx.doi.org/10.1016/j.acalib.2012.06.001.

Sobel, K., & Sugimoto, C. R. (2012). Assessment of learning during library instruction: practices, prevalence, and preparation. *The Journal of Academic Librarianship*, *38*(4), 191–204. http://dx.doi.org/10.1016/j.acalib.2012.04.004.

Spievak, E. R., & Hayes-Bohanan, P. (2013). Just enough of a good thing: indications of long-term efficacy in one-shot library instruction. *The Journal of Academic Librarianship*, *39*(6), 488–499. http://dx.doi.org/10.1016/j.acalib.2013.08.013.

Stowe, B. (2011). "I can't find anything": towards establishing a continuum in curriculum-integrated library instruction. *Reference Services Review*, *39*(1), 81–97.

Swoger, B. J. M. (2011). Closing the assessment loop using pre- and post-assessment. *Reference Services Review*, *39*(2), 244–259. http://dx.doi.org/10.1108/00907321111135475.

Tewell, E. C. (2014). Tying television comedies to information literacy: a mixed-methods investigation. *The Journal of Academic Librarianship*, *40*(2), 134–141. http://dx.doi.org/10.1016/j.acalib.2014.02.004.

Tucker, J. M. (1980). User education in academic libraries: a century in retrospect. *Library Trends*, *29*(1), 9–26.

Vecchione, A., & Mellinger, M. (2012). Using geolocation apps for academic library outreach and instruction. *Reference Librarian*, *53*(4), 415–423. http://dx.doi.org/10.1080/02763877.2012.704589.

Wang, Z. (2007). Smart spaces: creating new instructional space with smart classroom technology. *New Library World*, *109*(3–4), 150–165. http://dx.doi.org/10.1108/0307 4800810857603.

Watson, S. E., Rex, C., Markgraf, J., Kishel, H., Jennings, E., & Hinnant, K. (2013). Revising the "one-shot" through lesson study: collaborating with writing faculty to rebuild a library instruction session. *College & Research Libraries*, *74*(4), 381–398.

Weiner, S. A. (2012). Institutionalizing information literacy. *The Journal of Academic Librarianship*, *38*(5), 287–293. http://dx.doi.org/10.1016/j.acalib.2012.05.004.

Willson, R. (2012). Independent searching during one-shot information literacy instruction sessions: is it an effective use of time? *Evidence Based Library & Information Practice*, *7*(4), 52–67.

Zdravkovska, N., Cech, M., Beygo, P., & Kackley, B. (2010). Laser pointers: low-cost, low-tech innovative, interactive instruction tool. *Journal of Academic Librarianship*, *36*(5), 440–444.

Zhang, W. (2001). Building partnerships in liberal arts education: library team teaching. *Reference Services Review*, *29*(2), 141–149.

CHAPTER 3

Gaining Faculty Buy-in

3.1 THE HISTORY OF FACULTY–LIBRARIAN COLLABORATION

The academic library has always existed to assist faculty and students with instruction, learning, and research. As academic librarians increasingly see themselves as the appropriate teachers of information literacy (IL), collaborating with faculty becomes paramount. Along with faculty collaboration comes increased involvement with student learning, which could mean working with faculty to create assignments, teaching classes, planning courses, and designing curriculum. Ultimately, the success of IL programs depends on developing partnerships to integrate IL with class assignments and communicate to students that their professors value IL instruction as well (Anthony, 2010).

In more traditional universities, the faculty–library collaboration is an emerging phenomenon as these two entities are driven by separate agendas, teaching and providing information services, respectively. However, the rapid development of information and communication technologies has built a platform for these two institutions to work collaboratively and to create synergistic relationships (Wijayasundara, 2008).

With the introduction of certain technologies in the mid-1990s, there was a significant shift in student participation and faculty–librarian collaboration. At that time, computers were not used in library instruction and were usually only available in public areas of the library. There were also very few electronic databases available, and the librarian always conducted the search for a student. The librarian would provide printed handouts describing the complex computer search processes and would lecture students on the mechanics of searching the Educational Resources Information Center (ERIC) database. As can be expected, students did not fully comprehend, retain, or implement much of the information, perhaps partly due to

The Fortuitous Teacher
ISBN 978-0-08-100193-6

the method of delivery and the students' lack of familiarity with computers. As integration of technology within the library advanced, the librarian would then roll a computer into the classroom for instruction sessions. Students would receive a lecture on search strategies, supplemented with handouts. The class would then gather around the single computer to view an active search. The students were excited, because they were now able to see a demonstration of a computer search by the librarian in real time. The faculty member was usually silent during these earlier phases of technology integration in bibliographic instruction (BI) sessions, viewing this portion as the librarian's area of expertise, and to show respect to the librarian during delivery. Also at this time, most faculty members had limited computer skills, so simply were not able to assist with the sessions. Therefore, the collaboration between the faculty member and the librarian during BI sessions was minimal to nonexistent. The installation of computer labs in the library drastically shifted the teaching–learning process, because the students were now able to simultaneously execute searches along with the librarian's demonstration. However, the BI session was still scripted. The faculty member also began to actively collaborate in the teaching process, because for the first time there were multiple student computer stations to be monitored. At this point, the librarian and the faculty member began to communicate with each other about student progress and problems (Bhavnagri & Bielat, 2005).

Today, faculty–librarian partnerships are common. Collaborative projects may include collection development, website and subject guide development, as well as writing groups and teaching IL. IL instruction is by far the most widespread practice of collaboration between teaching faculty and librarians (Reynolds, Smith, & D'Silva, 2013). To develop these partnerships, it is vital to understand how faculty views the skills of librarians and how they can support teaching, learning, and research. However, certain factors such as under-use of information resources and scarce interaction between faculty and librarians can have a negative impact on collaborative efforts. In fact, relations between faculty and librarians can often be problematic and even tense. A study conducted at the University Institute of Lisbon

Libraries (ISCTE-IUL) in Portugal explored faculty perceptions of librarians. The study identifies the key variables affecting the willingness of faculty to collaborate with librarians and discusses the factors that faculty feels are most important to that relationship. The willingness of faculty to collaborate is impacted by the identification and understanding of IL needs, commitment to IL, and satisfaction of IL needs. It is recommended that IL librarians identify and understand faculty needs and develop better communication to encourage a positive view of librarians (Amante, Extremeño, & da Costa, 2013).

The findings of a 6-month research project which took a global perspective on the issue of library value focused on the relationships between academic libraries and academic departments. The aim of the project was to explore the value of academic libraries for teaching and research staff. Some institutions provided services that are usually regarded as being outside the normal remit of libraries. For example, at the University of Utah, the library provides teaching staff with a video production suite that they can use to create teaching content. The libraries at the Karolinska Institutet and Wake Forest University provide information technology tools for teaching staff, and help them to use and incorporate tools, such as podcasts, wikis, or web sites/blogs, in their courses. Purdue University has taken a proactive approach to research support, identifying research data management as an area that should be developed and supported by the library. However, staff capacity, poor communication, relationships with departments, as well as perceptions of the value of the academic library by teaching and research staff were found to be stumbling blocks. Some librarians felt that faculty did not want outside help for their research, considering themselves experts in their field. Faculty often relied on their research network for help and did not see librarians as a natural first point of contact for research help (Creaser & Spezi, 2014).

Librarians with faculty status often find that challenges about their role are eliminated and perceptions are shifted in that faculty often view them as equals and consult them more often with their research needs. Librarians are trying to move away from being seen solely as service providers, but rather as teaching and research partners, with more involvement in the curriculum and in the research activity of the institution. Creaser and Spezi's (2014) interviews with library managers indicate that teaching and research partnerships may lead to a renewed image, which would be a vital part of the repositioning of the library on campus. The challenge appears to be in getting the message across about what the modern academic library is about, and how librarians can help faculty in their teaching and research through instruction and research partnerships. However, even with instant and remote access to resources and services, faculty seems less aware of the library's role. There is also evidence that faculty do not always know how to utilize library services and the expertise of librarians despite the various communication channels libraries use to reach out to faculty.

At Sam Houston State University (SHSU), a history professor and history subject-specialist librarian experimented with an intensive approach to faculty–librarian collaboration. IL instruction was incorporated in an entire course syllabus from start to finish, with a consistent librarian coteaching presence and ongoing communication between both collaborators. The history professor found that collaboration with the librarian improved aspects of pedagogy, which better supported student needs. The professor, based on the evaluation of student assignments, was able to suggest new areas in which the librarian could develop new instructional support tools (Cassidy & Hendrickson, 2013).

Effective faculty–library collaboration is vital when it comes to imparting the necessary information skills to students. These collaborations are not always free of complications, such as librarians often being viewed as mere service providers and not teachers. This can lead to an imbalance in the relationship between faculty and librarians, in which the librarians usually know more about the role and needs of faculty than vice versa, and librarians being the only ones who find this imbalance problematic. However, the different backgrounds and perspectives held by librarians and teachers can be of real value to these collaborations and, in turn, to students. Not surprisingly, faculty and librarians often have differing opinions about the significance of collaboration, particularly with some instructors believing that IL must be learned "gradually and intuitively." Consequently, it is often difficult to gain institutional support for collaborative efforts. For those who do enter collaborative partnerships, trust, timing, willingness to share knowledge, and a shared understanding of purpose are all vital to the success of the collaboration (Øvern, 2014).

Librarians continue to discover new approaches to partnering with teaching faculty, for example, in English as a Second Language (ESL) departments. The Ohio State University Libraries (OSUL) have a successful program which was developed to encourage collaboration between classroom faculty and librarians. This program, and those similar to it, can help librarians and faculty move beyond the one-shot lecture model of library instruction to a more in-depth collaboration between the library and the classroom. At OSUL, this was particularly successful with an ESL course in which most international students had previously not been exposed to important concepts relating to copyright, use of citations, and academic plagiarism (Herring, 2014).

Collaboration has other benefits such as creating a dialog between two practitioners in two different disciplines, and as a result combining two bodies of scholarship and professional knowledge. Through this collaboration each is forced to look at their individual work and discipline in broader terms, and to ask larger questions related to student learning and the learning community in general. In any partnership, it is imperative to discover a common ground through conversation and dialog. Collaboration, like research and writing, is a process that has to start somewhere. Many collaborators begin by becoming aware of areas of shared interest and inquiry, and proceed from that point (Jacobs & Jacobs, 2009).

Meaningful collaboration in assessment of student success is also possible. At Colorado University (CU) Denver, three researchers from different areas within librarianship, academia, and the campus collaborated to explore the value of library services and resources in the college classroom. They found that comprehensive and meaningful assessment of student success is impossible in isolation. However, it is possible to cultivate a learning environment between student and instructor, student and librarian, and instructor and librarian. The CU

Denver study revealed the exciting possibilities when academic faculty and librarians move beyond established roles and responsibilities, and attempt student learning outcomes assessment from an interdisciplinary perspective (Pan, Ferrer-Vinent, & Bruehl, 2014).

Collaboration also works well between subject-specialist librarians and teaching faculty, for example, in designing library scavenger hunts to coordinate with current, timely assignments and information needs. Librarians and faculty who work together to design these types of assignments illustrate, time and again, that cooperation produces an effective teaching tool. By collaborating with teaching faculty, librarians can provide professors with the knowledge of current library resources for their students, preventing the types of scavenger hunts in which faculty suggest the use of outdated library resources (Rugan & Nero, 2013).

There have been collaborations between not only subject-specialist librarians, but also university archivists and instructors. It is actually not uncommon for archivists to collaborate with librarians. At Eastern Washington University, a document-based research course in the social sciences curriculum provided the opportunity for a unique collaboration between librarian subject specialists, the University Archivist, and the class instructor. First, the collaboration raised the visibility of the archives with students who otherwise might not have been aware of it. Second, the archivist was able to learn from the librarians, as well as gain valuable experience in large-group instruction. Finally, the collaboration broke down some of the barriers to collaboration that can exist within a library (Victor, Otto, & Mutschler, 2013).

At University of Wisconsin (UW)-Eau Claire, a lesson study was conducted starting in 2010 with the goal of overhauling the content of their one-shot library instruction sessions. In this process, the librarians were able to collaborate with cross-disciplinary faculty. Because of the collaborative nature of lesson study, it allowed the librarians to work closely with faculty as true partners in teaching. Generally, a lesson study is done by collaborative groups of teachers who begin by examining textbooks, standards, and current methods for relaying essential concepts to students in a single lesson. Teachers usually then plan, observe, and analyze actual classroom lessons, using assessment results for the design of future lessons and for teaching and learning in general. Specifically, lesson study is an examination of practice that challenges teachers to examine their goals for a lesson, as well as student response to them (Watson et al., 2013).

IL cannot be taught in isolation; it requires a connection to the teaching and learning occurring in the classroom. In light of this, collaboration between librarians and faculty members becomes paramount. This type of collaboration has several important features, such as mutual goals, mutual respect, advanced planning, and substantive contributions by both parties for designing instructional goals and activities and then carrying them out (Donham & Green, 2004).

3.2 THE IMPORTANCE OF FACULTY COLLABORATION

The history of faculty–librarian collaboration has shown the origins of the challenges that still exist today. Librarians can tackle these challenges by drawing on different fields of expertise and developing innovative strategic alliances in the academic community. To develop alliances librarians must first have a thorough understanding of how faculty view librarian skills and the role they play in supporting teaching, learning, and research. Faculty with a positive view of the skills of librarians and their contribution to teaching, learning, and research tend to have greater trust in librarians and the services provided by libraries. In fact, the greater the amount of trust and commitment faculty have in librarians and libraries results in increased willingness of faculty to collaborate with librarians (Amante et al., 2013). Indeed, a strong librarian–faculty alliance is a great way to improve the delivery of education, the promotion of IL, and the creation of a university-wide approach to academic service in general (Anthony, 2010).

Interestingly, faculty-initiated collaborations are more powerful than librarian-initiated or officially mandated attempts. If the idea of collaboration comes from the faculty members, they are, of course, ready and receptive. They take ownership of the collaboration. However, in time, they must come into alignment with the IL agenda of the librarian. Good faculty candidates for collaboration usually reveal themselves as such by indicating how their classroom goals and content are compatible with IL outcomes (Shane, 2004). Some librarians are finding that the boundaries between the roles of librarian and faculty are blurring, which has had the positive result of seamless content delivery to students. The hope is that extended, long-term collaboration will result in even greater benefits to all involved, whether for faculty, librarians, or students (Bhavnagri & Bielat, 2005).

Collaboration may mean maintaining on going contact between the instructor and librarian to exchange ideas, discuss challenges and experiences with students, as well as reevaluate and modify the course as needed. Instructors find that collaboration increases awareness of student confusion with assignment instructions through feedback from the librarian regarding repeated related questions from students. The instructor can more carefully define or demonstrate certain concepts in course lessons and assignment instructions, being sure not to assume preexisting student comprehension of concepts such as archives (Cassidy & Hendrickson, 2013). In this way faculty can learn from the librarians and gain experience in large-group instruction settings. In general, collaboration raises the visibility of information resources with students who otherwise might not have been exposed to them and also helps break down some of the barriers that can exist within a library (Victor et al., 2013).

In turn, librarians find that the professor's evaluation of student assignments helps with suggestions of new areas in which the librarian can develop instructional support tools. For example, identifying a need for a guide about how to evaluate the feasibility of a research project and how to become familiar with the research and writing approach of a specific discipline (Cassidy & Hendrickson, 2013). Communication with faculty is essential to moving library instruction and research support services forward, allowing librarians to have greater insight into the teaching and research needs of faculty (Creaser & Spezi, 2014). In collaborating with distance learning specialists, including instructional designers, librarians can provide reference services and deliver relevant instructional content in the online environment. Instructional designers often become advocates for the inclusion of libraries and information resources in distance education courses. In this environment, librarians provide the necessary expertise to integrate IL instruction with these courses in ways that are meaningful and seamless (Frank & Howell, 2003).

In the distance learning community, establishing a comprehensive collaboration between both academic faculty and administration staff is critical for librarians to make library resources and services available and applicable to online students. Though challenging, it is vital for academic librarians to embrace new information technologies and to carry out their collaborative role utilizing these rapidly developing technologies to enhance library service while keeping pace with the exploding arena of online education (Fang, 2006).

Some librarians feel that true collaboration means moving beyond the one-shot lecture model of library instruction to the course level. At this level, both the librarian and instructor have an increased ability to identify long-term goals, use various technologies and teaching techniques to convey course content, as well as employ assessment techniques to determine the value of the program. For this type of collaboration to be successful, the instructor and librarian must be motivated, purposeful, and have clear-cut mutual objectives. Of course, on going assessment allows for the modification of course content to best meet the needs of students and accommodate different learning styles (Herring, 2014).

The point can be made that the most important result of collaboration is the conversation that is ignited between faculty members and librarians. It often leads to discussions about application to different courses and disciplines and incites ideas for more collaboration across campus, which in turn can impact teaching practices. Collaboration leads to the discovery of common ground through dialog and conversation (Jacobs & Jacobs, 2009). On the other hand, the different backgrounds and perspectives held by librarians and instructors can be of real value to the collaboration and, by extension, to students. Very often, these differences are often downplayed; however, they can give collaboration an extra dimension in which collaborators can learn from each other (Øvern, 2014). Collaboration can even impact the purchasing of new resources based on the research interests of faculty, and how they use various databases (Reynolds et al., 2013).

Initial discussions preceding collaboration allow for the creation of a variety of choices for library instruction so that faculty members may decide which concepts they would like to be included in a library session. Faculty are able to discover what can realistically be covered in a 50-min session. Providing these options to meet the IL needs of students gives an alternate approach to fulfilling faculty requests and student needs at the same time (Watson et al., 2013).

Wijayasundara (2008) stated that collaboration allows for the creation of library instruction programs geared toward individual class needs. Also, working collaboratively increases the likelihood of creating high-quality products and services at a lower cost compared to working individually. For both faculty and students it also leads to higher-quality research and improved literature reviews. With the bringing together of diverse knowledge, experience, and skills, collaboration increases motivation of learners and instructors, leading to increased reflection, innovation, and scope of content. Instructional librarians are charged with keeping faculty and students current with information resources and services. Ultimately, these efforts increase knowledge of information skills, fostering lifelong learning and leading to better overall use of information. Even more challenging are the collaborative efforts to design assignments aiding development of higher-order thinking and IL skills and competencies (Shane, 2004).

Collaboration also leads to increased faculty support of librarians. Faculty members who have positive feelings about librarians and the library are more likely to use library services, whether in the library, in their offices, or even at home. As use of library services by classroom faculty increases, administrative support for library services will remain stable or possibly even increase. In fact, faculty who feel good about the library and librarians are more likely to encourage their students to use the library. Another positive aspect of collaboration is the promotion and support of faculty research, which also allows librarians to participate in the scholarly process. When the working relationship between faculty and librarians is less than positive, miscommunication, tension, and even failed projects can occur (Kotter, 1999). The challenge for the librarian is to show faculty how to integrate resources with their classroom needs by providing specific library workshops to help make their courses successful (Tillman, 2008).

Cardwell (2001) observes that good relationships between faculty and librarians often spill over to reference desk service. Faculty members who are familiar with the librarians and confident in their abilities and willingness to help are more likely to encourage students to ask for help at the desk. This leads to better reference service, increased opportunities to pursue collaborative projects, participation in campus-wide initiatives, and opportunities to pursue professional development. Librarians can gain many benefits from collaboration, such as the opportunity to learn from experienced faculty to become better teachers, which leads to providing better instructional services to students. Collaboration also reduces librarians' isolation and increases their sense of accomplishment. It allows them to develop long-term partnerships with classroom faculty in promoting IL skills to the campus academic community (Zhang, 2001).

At the University of Delaware library, instructional sessions for a senior-level class were expanded into a program of continuous faculty–librarian support for students completing the class project. Students benefitted by gaining access to improved choices of resources and greater awareness of the published research in their subject areas. Although the proposals initially submitted by students had a tendency to be unfocused, suggestions from the professor and librarian helped them to refocus their topics, and increased their confidence in their ability to complete the assignment. It also aided in their understanding of the research process and increased enthusiasm for their work (Stein & Lamb, 1998).

Sanborn (2005) discusses faculty–librarian collaboration at St. Paul's School, a college in New Hampshire. The creation of unique IL sessions provided students with research skills they could immediately utilize. As a result of well-researched student papers, there was increase in student willingness to contact the reference librarian after attending a session. Through improvement in the content, quality, and meaningfulness of the library instruction sessions, student library and research skills also improved. St. Paul's School found that library instruction is more effective when combined with faculty collaboration.

Librarians at Eastern Kentucky University found that collaboration has a positive impact on teaching faculty for several reasons. Faculty members are more motivated to evaluate resources prior to designing an assignment, which in turn equates to higher-quality student products. They also gain assistance with their workload, if they are willing to take advantage of the skills of librarians. It helps them to refer students to the library with confidence, and break up the monotony of the regular class schedule. Students also benefit from enhanced collection development in the faculty member's subject area. The positive impact of collaboration on students is most evident as assignments are usually better planned and become more meaningful to them. This is due, in part, to IL being integrated with the curriculum. Information becomes more relevant to their lives, and they develop a respect for intellectual property. They also cultivate the critical thinking skills needed to evaluate resources, develop intellectual curiosity, and become independent learners (Cooper & Gardner, 2001).

Beyond the benefits to students and faculty, collaboration has a positive impact on the broader campus community. Students do better work overall because expectations for learning are raised. In fact, library services often serve as a recruitment tool for potential faculty and students. Generally, when the library is at the center of the campus community, the social and cultural implications are evident, and interdisciplinary approaches are more highly valued. In addition, employees have increased access to specialized information. Ultimately, the library enjoys increased campus visibility (Cooper & Gardner, 2001).

It is highly evident that there are numerous benefits to faculty–librarian collaboration. Generally, it allows librarians and faculty to develop meaningful assignments and classroom experiences that are designed to teach or reinforce one or more IL competencies. It reinforces the positive relationship between students and librarians, as well as the importance of the librarian's role. It also helps to blend the subject content with information research and evaluation skills. Librarians and faculty are able to mutually reinforce IL skills through active-learning strategies (Gandhi, 2005).

3.3 WINNING STRATEGIES FOR GAINING FACULTY BUY-IN

Increased faculty buy-in and participation in IL sessions results in improved student performance. Of course, faculty should always be consulted regarding the needs of their students. However, to ensure student participation faculty can link student performance to their course grade, for example, by incorporating a quiz to be completed. This has been shown to improve both faculty and student buy-in. The marketing strategy for IL sessions and their related resources is essential to informing both faculty and students of their availability (Ergood, Padron, & Rebar, 2012).

Although marketing will increase faculty awareness of library resources and expose faculty to the myriad of library services, librarians are reminded to recognize faculty work pressures by creating convenient ways for instructors to learn more about library innovations. Tying these activities to professional development credit for faculty is a great motivator for faculty to explore library resources. Librarians can create web-based library guides specifically for adjunct faculty that presents a quick overview, an invitation to explore library services further. Library guides are easy to update and allow librarians to gauge faculty interests and gain faculty feedback. Essentially, they allow faculty to quickly see the range of library resources available for instruction. Library liaisons are encouraged to meet with faculty one-on-one to explore ways to integrate library innovations into class assignments. Tying attendance of these meetings to professional development credit gives faculty great impetus to participate. It is also important for librarians to present workshops relevant to faculty objectives for increasing student retention and success. The highlighting of new and emerging technologies is a good place to start, redefining where, when, and how students learn. Focusing on technology encourages faculty to see the library as more than just a building and view librarians as tech savvy colleagues (Virtue & Esparza, 2013).

Lucas (2011) discusses faculty receiving in-service training sessions to introduce new and existing faculty to library resources and services. These sessions can serve to market the library and its services and also highlight librarians' teaching and research skills. Not only do they demonstrate how the library supports faculty and students who are conducting research and writing, but they give librarians the chance to showcase their professional abilities and research experience. Faculty in-service sessions can promote library research assistance and market services such as student-based library instruction group sessions; the availability of library subscription-based online databases; free web-based Internet sites, such as PubMed and Google Scholar; and services such as interlibrary loan, collection development, reserves, and archives. Inevitably, faculty will market the in-service sessions to other faculty members through word of mouth, driving up the number of sessions provided. In fact, in-service sessions are considered part of the library's overall marketing plan to explain where the library is and where it is heading. Generally, these types of sessions increase faculty support of the library and in turn elevate usage statistics in reference desk activity, library instruction, interlibrary loan, and reserves. They also help to improve the library's image and encourage collaboration between librarians and faculty.

At Emporia State University (ESU), credit-bearing professional development courses emphasizing electronic databases were organized and delivered to academic faculty in the fall 1995 and spring 1996 semesters. Although the courses themselves became an effective public relations and marketing tool, librarians noticed overall an enhanced positive image of the library across campus due to librarians taking on the role of teacher and facilitators of learning. As formal teachers, librarians were able to interact with participants as colleagues, highlighting the various services and resources available to the students, faculty, and staff of ESU, and presenting the Library Electronic Classroom as a model for instructional technology. Librarians noticed a direct correlation between faculty interest in these courses and subsequent requests for library instruction using the very same databases showcased in the professional development courses. Faculty participants also contacted the Coordinator of Library Instruction for general sessions in the Library Electronic Classroom for their students as a direct result of attending the professional development course (Akers, Martin, & Summey, 2000).

In the late 1990s, George Washington University's Melvin Gelman Library instituted a number of then-innovative strategies to gain faculty buy-in, such as electronic lists, e-mail accounts, faculty brown-bag workshops, library guides, and faculty focus groups. In fact, the university library created the position of faculty outreach librarian to educate faculty about the growing role of information technology in research and teaching, and to enhance their support for new electronic resources (Stebelman, Siggins, & Nutty, 1999).

Partnering with discipline-based classroom faculty forms strategic alliances that advance library instruction goals and garner faculty support. Along with this, librarians can focus on working with first-year students in courses, such as discipline-based English composition classes, which emphasize competence in the use of library resources. Further, developing credit-bearing library instruction courses for first-year students as an integral part of their undergraduate core curriculum allows for even greater collaboration with faculty and improves student retention rates (Rockman, 2002).

Many librarians report a sense of increased collegiality resulting from conducting training sessions for faculty. Librarians, as information specialists, are aware of the newest databases, and should take advantage of any opportunity to showcase their expertise to faculty and offer their support when needed. Indeed, faculty often observes that their students are more database savvy than they are, yet still see the need to make IL a priority for their students. They frequently recognize that journals, library catalogs, and indexes, mostly electronic now, have become so complex that their own research may be hindered by their lack of knowledge of the nuances of navigating new information tools. By helping faculty to learn how to navigate the complexities of these new information tools, librarians can position themselves as the appropriate information experts to help them with these tools. Although this may seem like a simple tactical maneuver, it actually represents a genuine contribution from a position of strength, a contribution that no one except an academic librarian can make. If faculty are made aware of what academic librarians can do for them, they may also be convinced that their students need to benefit from this expertise as well (Badke, 2005).

Kempcke (2002) discusses other effective ways to promote IL, such as through the collection of data on its benefits and then development of an implementation plan involving faculty. Surveys can be used to make other faculty aware of IL and how the teaching of IL skills can benefit them and also their students. Teaching IL leads to curriculum reform, a stronger sense of institutional identity, greater faculty satisfaction, increased enrollment, higher levels of student retention and performance, and an improved public profile for the university, which can all attract faculty and administrators to the library's cause. The degree to which librarians' skills and activities are seen as important is connected to how intertwined they are with the university system. Therefore, as the librarian's influence increases, the direct and indirect benefits to the academic library also increase. The more successfully we address critical problems with IL, the more likely we are to gain stature and attract an appropriate distribution of university resources.

Similarly, the Claremont Colleges Library Instruction Services Department developed a quiz that could be integrated into the learning management software to accompany a local online, open-source IL tutorial. The quiz was integrated into individual course pages, allowing students to receive a grade for completion and improving faculty and student buy-in (Lowe, Booth, Tagge, & Stone, 2014).

The librarians at Northwest Vista College realized that for IL to succeed, librarians must have the support and respect of the teaching faculty. They determined that if faculty were aware of the information resources available to them through the library they would be more likely to send their classes to the library for instruction. Keeping faculty members informed about library resources resulted in their sending students to the library for library instruction, which allowed the students to become familiar with and comfortable using the library. This faculty outreach was conducted via special faculty workshops, creating online forms, placing special links on the library web page, and increased contact and collaboration in general (Reeves, Nishimuta, McMillan, & Godin, 2003). Similarly, at Northridge Oviatt Library of California State University, librarians made efforts to reach out to campus faculty through streaming video communication, marketing new and existing library resources and services to academia. They found that marketing the library to faculty through 1-min videos was a fantastic opportunity for dialog, especially because the librarians collaborated with faculty themselves in developing the video campaign (Martin, 2012).

According to Meulemans and Carr (2013), no amount of marketing or superficial outreach will help to create the partnerships with faculty if instructional librarians fail to engage faculty in a collaborative manner. They examine how librarians and faculty can become genuine partners in student learning and move toward the common goal of getting students to think critically. Librarians are encouraged to initiate more collaborative conversations with professors, establishing partnerships and shifting away from a service orientation to a true partnership in student learning. These partnerships are essential for effective instruction and require the professor and librarian to work together to achieve the common goal of creating learning opportunities for students. Although librarians and instructors have the same desired outcomes for students, it is the librarian that has the greater task of articulating how they can contribute to the creation of meaningful learning opportunities for students.

Specifically targeting part-time faculty for collaboration is another great way to reach students because of their pivotal role in teaching "gatekeeper" courses associated with IL learning outcomes. Part-time faculty, though often overlooked, should be viewed as equally important as their full-time colleagues. They can serve as a bridge between academic libraries and the students they teach, and can help to decrease the existing part-time faculty "disconnect." This type of collaboration will facilitate student IL skills, as well as improve student retention rates (Klentzin & Bucci, 2012).

At some academic libraries these types of collaborations are used to establish a base of reference support for each course across the college curriculum. Librarians collaborate with and support faculty on a college campus to reinforce overall academic success and seek out the latest strategies to support this collaboration, with the goal of delivering an effective and productive experience to cultivate student course work. Simply enhancing communication and interaction with the faculty supports students' reference needs. Actively engaging in shared consultation with the faculty ensures that the appropriate reference resources are available to students. Materials that are selected to support a specific course through this type of close collaboration may more effectively narrow down the exact materials required to achieve student success in a course than those selected without it (Massis, 2012).

The Utah State University, Merrill–Cazier Library instruction program conducted an 8-week summer IL workshop to strengthen collaborative relationships between faculty and librarians. Although the library already had a close relationship with the Writing Program, this in-depth collaboration strengthened those relationships and improved librarians' and lecturers' ability to speak to everyone's concerns and ideas as a collective, rather than as two separate groups. The participants consisted of highly motivated instructors and librarians who sincerely desired to work together to improve student learning. The often-isolated instructors highly valued the meeting and discussion time, feeling that the librarians demonstrated an understanding of their needs. As well, the coordinating librarians felt valued and respected by the instructors. Because the majority of the workshop focused on student issues, rather than those of the librarians, lecturers were more open to helping librarians rewrite IL goals and more agreeable to incorporating librarians into more areas of their lesson plans. This shared focus on how best to teach students helped avoid the situation in which librarians felt they must demand respect from instructors, rather than simply collaborate on an equal footing. In this case, lecturers and librarians played equal roles in contributing to design outcomes, assignments, and activities for the IL instruction. The relatively casual workshop environment and collaborative nature of the endeavor relieved any tension that might exist when librarians adopt roles that blur the lines between instruction and librarianship (Lundstrom, Fagerheim, & Benson, 2014).

Faculty support is essential for any course-integrated program of library instruction to succeed. It takes time to build a partnership and mutual support between a department and the library, and longevity on the part of both library personnel and the teaching faculty is helpful. By regularly attending faculty meetings, librarians can integrate the library, and especially instruction, into the fabric of daily discussions about curriculum and an entire program. New faculty can be introduced to a department in which IL is an integral aspect of the overall education mission. Although not all areas of a curriculum may currently participate in IL instruction, the college's endorsement of any program in which IL is central makes a much more stable environment for consistent inclusion of the library in the overall learning process. Only supportive faculty can truly help students to realize that what they are doing is important (Christensen, 2004).

3.4 PLANNING INSTRUCTIONAL SESSIONS WITH FACULTY

When planning instructional sessions, it is beneficial for librarians to see themselves as colleagues of faculty, equals and allies in student learning rather than as guest lecturers, sideshows, or academic support. Having regular conversations with faculty about their students' work is encouraged, which can include asking to see papers or projects students are turning in. Asking faculty if they are satisfied with their students' work can provide an opportunity to offer knowledge and expertise and to be viewed as a colleague. At times, students will ask librarians to explain aspects of assignments unrelated to IL instruction, which provides another opportunity for librarians to approach faculty to discuss the issue and work toward a solution. Faculty members who are open to new avenues to improve student learning will listen, as well as discuss these issues with other faculty members. This will inevitably lead to stronger collegial alliances between faculty and librarians, benefitting the teaching environment as a whole, as librarians help faculty to design IL-based assignments (Oakleaf et al., 2012).

At Indiana Institute of Technology's McMillen Library, academic librarians work with faculty to design fun, interactive library instruction sessions that align closely with student needs. These sessions are also scheduled based on specific faculty and course needs. The reality is that much of the faculty may be oblivious of the different services offered by the library, so it is important to share past experiences with faculty when designing assignments. The sessions include project-based learning activities that encourage student engagement and collaboration, while incorporating IL, critical thinking, and technology skills. The librarians usually request that faculty schedule library instruction 1 week in advance. However, project-based learning activities can take more time, up to a year in advance, to plan and coordinate. Librarians need this time to incorporate IL and lifelong learning skills into classroom activities, whereas faculty need time to adjust their course curriculum and schedule for these types of activities. Although these activities can take a considerable amount of time to develop, students benefit from a highly interactive approach, which can be seen in an increase in postlibrary instruction evaluation scores (Ringle, 2014). Trusted resources chosen collaboratively by librarians and faculty lead to a higher comfort level for students, and the ability to build on strengths in their subsequent years at the institution. Additionally, if the faculty has been actively engaged prior to the start of an IL class, these trusted resources can be used effectively in most any course going forward (Massis, 2012).

In 2010 the McIntyre Library and the English Department at the University of Wisconsin–Eau Claire began a partnership to alleviate the dual issue of one-shot library instruction, that is, the overstuffed nature of the lessons and the lack of collaborative, interdisciplinary input in designing and running them. They accomplished this through a relatively new mode of inquiry in American education: the lesson study. Librarians and English faculty at one college campus confronted these challenges by participating in a year-long lesson study, a process of collaboratively planning, observing, and assessing a single lesson. They collectively identified goals and priorities, at the same time designing and redesigning the lesson as necessary (Watson et al., 2013).

This team-teaching approach starts with a meeting between the instructor and librarian, in which learning objectives and assignments are discussed. This meeting is vital as it lays the foundation for the collaboration. It is important that both librarian and teacher take full ownership of the activity and believe in the objectives and the method. The librarian and teacher decide on a plan for the teaching activities, for example, which of them will cover certain subjects. Once team-teaching is executed, the teacher and librarian collaborate on assessment and further planning. Team-teaching can be performed as a single-session activity, part of a whole course or an entire semester. This will depend on the nature of the course and the needs of the students. The team-teaching approach can be used on all class sizes (Øvern, 2014).

From the faculty member's perspective, he or she must take into account the impact that IL sessions can have on teaching and on assignment design. Although he or she may think that the class assignment has already been well developed, it could possibly appear vague to the students. After participating in IL sessions in which a librarian taught students the specific research skills to complete the assignment, many faculty members are prompted to rethink what they want their students to achieve with the assignment, that is, the end goal of their research process. Both the librarians and the faculty agree that even one IL session in a semester is more beneficial to students than no session at all (Hoffmann & Adams, 2012).

The Library Instruction Services unit at University of Texas integrates faculty collaboration by contacting faculty members individually to offer their services. The resulting faculty collaboration takes various forms, such as working with the faculty to assist them with developing the course over time, conducting one-shot instruction sessions while using course guides related to a specific assignment, and creating exercises and assignments which teach specific IL learning outcomes, and at the same time supporting the course curriculum. For example, in one journalism class, an assignment and guide was created to show students how to find articles from three different types of newspapers, and to analyze how audience and cultural context impact news reporting (Ostrow, 2010).

Librarians and graduate instructors at the University of Windsor's Leddy Library were paired for both semesters of the academic year, meeting in pairs and working closely to teach the research process and to help students to complete a particular assignment. The collaboration shifted from focusing solely on the library sessions to conversations, relationships, and learning communities that developed progressively over the course of the year. This collaborative model helped them to think more effectively about how to approach the teaching of research, as well as the specific research component of the composition course. The particular assignment and activities that came out of this collaboration were possible only through the input from both the library and the composition program. Together they were able to create a much more integrated assignment for students. The resulting assignment was much more effective than the one created by the library or the composition program alone (Jacobs & Jacobs, 2009). When assisting faculty with creating library-related assignments, librarians can target specific resources within a certain discipline. This can be especially useful in introductory courses for subjects such as English and psychology (Simons, 2009).

When working collaboratively to create assignments for one-shot library sessions, librarians can begin by working with faculty who know and trust their observations about student experiences, focusing on those faculty who may be disappointed with students' general research papers. It may be wise to take the opportunity to suggest updating the assignment by offering to help create a new assignment. This can become a fluid partnership in which students' responses to the new assignment are compared to the previous assignment. Generally, it may be more effective in the long run to begin collaborative efforts with one or two faculty members in one-shot sessions, than to try to immediately effect broader changes across the entire campus (Kelly, 2014).

Librarians at one college library in the United Arab Emirates found that faculty collaboration was integral to the success of their program. Because the teachers were the most familiar with their students' English language skills and individual learning styles, they were the best qualified to review and test the IL activity before releasing it to the students. This allowed the library staff to make changes based on feedback from faculty about whether the activities and language were appropriate for the students' level and also correlated to the curriculum. Working with the instructors to develop the IL matrices and activities began with an understanding of the foundational learning outcomes, which then led to the creation of the IL learning outcomes. Instructors were asked to review the learning outcomes before any activities were actually created to determine whether they were appropriate for their respective levels. Once this was completed, they were also asked to provide a list of the weekly topics or textbook themes that they were currently teaching. The goal of the librarians was to tie IL activities as closely as possible to these themes to better integrate IL into the curriculum (Johnston & Marsh, 2014). When incorporating new activities into class sessions, a good strategy is to meet about a week before a scheduled class to discuss the development of the lesson plan with the new activity. If the instructor is nervous about incorporating the new activity, they can plan to have the librarian either lead the activity, team-teach, or offer roving support by working with student groups (Finley, Skarl, Cox, & VanderPol, 2005).

The McIntyre Library of the University of Wisconsin–Eau Claire partnered with the English Department with the goal of creating a template that could be modified for varying research topics and class needs. This was accompanied by a detailed description which gave instructors a realistic sense of what was achievable in a one-shot instructional session. The librarians sought to identify the main goals of this session and had several weekly meetings with the instructors. During these meetings they discussed what these goals meant, how they might be demonstrated, and what could be accomplished in a 50-min class session. Coming to the realization that the initial list of goals was too ambitious for such a short class period, they narrowed the goals. They also identified a single overarching outcome, which was that students should be able to develop and conduct search strategies with an awareness of the search systems available to them. The main focus was to tie instruction to the stated goals, integrating active learning techniques, and including effective search examples (Watson et al., 2013).

Being able to speak effectively to faculty is essential for true collaboration. University of Arizona (UA) librarians created staff development workshops that provided strategies and tools for talking to faculty. Most librarians know from anecdotal evidence that instructors are not always satisfied with the quality of research their students find, but not many instructors seem to acknowledge that the problem may be with the way the assignment is organized and presented rather than with the students. To address this, the UA librarians developed five questions for librarians to ask instructors when collaborating to analyze a class assignment. The questions allow librarians and instructors to create the assignment with student success in mind, as well as to understand the obstacles to successful completion of the assignment. They can also determine which parts of the assignment students will most likely need help with while completing it. The questions also address instructor awareness of IL requirements, and how librarians can help them to acquire that knowledge (Hook, Stowell Bracke, Greenfield, & Mills 2003).

During the staff development workshops, participants were introduced to the idea of analyzing assignments in relation to the IL skills or knowledge required for students to complete them. The assignments would need to be examined for what help the professor might need to ensure that the assignment would be successful for their students. Strategies for speaking with instructors about assignments were discussed, particularly those assignments that are problematic for the students. Suggestions were shared for what to say to instructors and ideas about how to more fully develop those parts of the assignment. The team also suggested that when speaking with faculty about assignments, librarians first ask about the learning goals of the assignment. If any of the activities in an assignment do not help students reach those goals, then librarians can make suggestions about how instructors can modify or limit the assignment. In this way, the students can spend their time focusing on meeting the learning goals of the assignment (Hook et al., 2003).

At Villanova University's Falvey Memorial Library the planning group for the instruction program consisted of seven members: three general biology faculty members, a general biology laboratory coordinator, and three librarians, which included the past and present liaisons to the biology department and the library instructional coordinator. The initial meetings were mainly an open discussion to determine the collective goals of the program. They determined that the main goal was to increase the scientific literacy of students and provide them with the opportunity to find, evaluate, organize, and accurately communicate information about a specific topic in the sciences. With this ultimate goal in mind, they developed certain objectives for the research skills instructional session. They would introduce major library resources and science databases to early undergraduates so that they would immediately benefit from this familiarity. Then they would link the instruction to a specific project that provides an opportunity to practice and reinforce newly acquired research skills. Through this practical experience students learned about the various types of scientific literature, and were able to distinguish between scientific sources and the popular press. Students were guided through the process of efficiently using bibliographic databases, which includes the ability to select, search, and retrieve sources from a database. Students were also given guidelines for critically evaluating websites and other electronic sources with criteria such as authority, currency, bias, and relevancy. Working collaboratively in this way to design student assignments benefits students, faculty, and librarians (Bowden & DiBenedetto, 2001).

Seeking greater collaboration with faculty members provides opportunities for librarians to meaningfully engage with them through instructional assessment and assignment design. Not only is the resulting student assignment more substantial, but librarians are able to examine and analyze student performance with the faculty member, and further redesign the instruction and assignments for the next term (Oakleaf et al., 2012).

REFERENCES

Akers, C., Martin, N., & Summey, T. (2000). Teaching the teachers: library instruction through professional development courses. *Research Strategies, 17*(2–3), 215–221. http://dx.doi.org/10.1016/S0734-3310(00)00048-3.

Amante, M. J., Extremeño, A. I., & da Costa, A. F. (2013). Modelling variables that contribute to faculty willingness to collaborate with librarians: the case of the University Institute of Lisbon (ISCTE-IUL), Portugal. *Journal of Librarianship and Information Science, 45*(2), 91–102. http://dx.doi.org/10.1177/0961000612457105.

Anthony, K. (2010). Reconnecting the disconnects: library outreach to faculty as addressed in the literature. *College and Undergraduate Libraries, 17*(1), 79–92. http://dx.doi.org/10.1080/10691310903584817.

Badke, W. B. (2005). Can't get no respect: helping faculty to understand the educational power of information literacy. *Reference Librarian, 43*(89/90), 63–80. http://dx.doi.org/10.1300/J120v43n89_05.

Bhavnagri, N. P., & Bielat, V. (2005). Faculty-librarian collaboration to teach research skills: electronic symbiosis. *Reference Librarian, 43*(89/90), 121–138. http://dx.doi.org/10.1300/J120v43n89_09.

Bowden, T. S., & DiBenedetto, A. (2001). Information literacy in a biology laboratory session: an example of librarian–faculty collaboration. *Research Strategies*, *18*(2), 143–149. http://dx.doi.org/10.1016/S0734-3310(02)00071-X.

Cardwell, C. (2001). Faculty. *The Reference Librarian*, *35*(73), 253–263. http://dx.doi.org/10.1300/J120v35n73_03.

Cassidy, E. D., & Hendrickson, K. E. (2013). Faculty–librarian micro-level collaboration in an online graduate history course. *Journal of Academic Librarianship*, *39*(6), 458–463. http://dx.doi.org/10.1016/j.acalib.2013.08.018.

Christensen, B. (2004). Warp, weft, and waffle: weaving information literacy into an under-graduate music curriculum. *Notes—Quarterly Journal of the Music Library Association*, *60*(3), 616–631.

Cooper, C., & Gardner, B. (2001). Coming full circle: a library's adventure in collaboration with teaching faculty at Eastern Kentucky University. *Kentucky Libraries*, *65*(3), 23–25.

Creaser, C., & Spezi, V. (2014). Improving perceptions of value to teaching and research staff: the next challenge for academic libraries. *Journal of Librarianship and Information Science*, *46*(3), 191–206. http://dx.doi.org/10.1177/0961000613477678.

Donham, J., & Green, C. W. (2004). Perspectives on…developing a culture of collaboration: librarian as consultant. *The Journal of Academic Librarianship*, *30*(4), 314–321. http://dx.doi.org/10.1016/j.acalib.2004.04.005.

Ergood, A., Padron, K., & Rebar, L. (2012). Making library screencast tutorials: factors and processes. *Internet Reference Services Quarterly*, *17*(2), 95–107. http://dx.doi.org/10.1080/10875301.2012.725705.

Fang, X. S. (2006). Collaborative role of the academic librarian in distance learning—analysis on an information literacy tutorial in WebCT. *Electronic Journal of Academic and Special Librarianship*, *7*(2). http://southernlibrarianship.icaap.org/content/v07n02/fang_x01.htm.

Finley, P., Skarl, S., Cox, J., & VanderPol, D. (2005). Enhancing library instruction with peer planning. *Reference Services Review*, *33*(1), 112–122.

Frank, D. G., & Howell, E. (2003). New relationships in academe: opportunities for vitality and relevance. *College and Research Libraries News*, *64*(1), 24–27.

Gandhi, S. (2005). Faculty-librarian collaboration to assess the effectiveness of a five-session library instruction model. *Community and Junior College Libraries*, *12*(4), 15–48. http://dx.doi.org/10.1300/J107v12n04_05.

Herring, D. N. (2014). A purposeful collaboration: using a library course enhancement grant program to enrich ESL instruction. *Reference Librarian*, *55*(2), 128–143. http://dx.doi.org/10.1080/02763877.2014.880317.

Hoffmann, D., & Adams, V. (2012). Faculty/librarian collaboration: a faculty perspective on information literacy instruction. *Codex*, *2*(1), 25–35.

Hook, S. J., Stowell Bracke, M., Greenfield, L., & Mills, V. A. (2003). In-house training for instruction librarians. *Research Strategies*, *19*(2), 99–127. http://dx.doi.org/10.1016/j.resstr.2003.12.001.

Jacobs, H. L. M., & Jacobs, D. (2009). Transforming the one-shot library session into peda-gogical collaboration: information literacy and the English composition class. *Reference and User Services Quarterly*, *49*(1), 72–82.

Johnston, N., & Marsh, S. (2014). Using iBooks and iPad apps to embed information literacy into an EFL foundations course. *New Library World*, *115*(1/2), 51.

Kelly, S. L. (2014). Librarians, renounce the research paper! Using rhetoric to improve assign-ment design. *College and Undergraduate Libraries*, *21*(1), 90–98. http://dx.doi.org/10.1080/10691316.2014.877741.

Kempcke, K. (2002). The art of war for librarians: academic culture, curriculum reform, and wisdom from Sun Tzu. *Portal: Libraries and the Academy*, *2*(4), 529–551.

Klentzin, J. C., & Bucci, D. T. (2012). Part-time faculty and the academic library: a case study. *The Journal of Academic Librarianship, 38*(2), 101–107. http://dx.doi.org/10.1016/j.acalib.2012.02.002.

Kotter, W. R. (1999). Bridging the great divide: improving relations between librarians and classroom faculty. *Journal of Academic Librarianship, 25*(4), 294–303. http://dx.doi.org/10.1016/S0099-1333(99)80030-5.

Lowe, M. S., Booth, C., Tagge, N., & Stone, S. (2014). Integrating an information literacy quiz into the learning management system. *Communications in Information Literacy, 8*(1), 115–130.

Lucas, D. (2011). Faculty in-service: how to boost academic library services. *Collaborative Librarianship, 3*(2), 117–122.

Lundstrom, K., Fagerheim, B. A., & Benson, E. (2014). Librarians and instructors developing student learning outcomes: using frameworks to lead the process. *Reference Services Review, 42*(3), 484–498. http://dx.doi.org/10.1108/RSR-04-2014-0007.

Martin, C. M. (2012). One-minute video: marketing your library to faculty. *Reference Services Review, 40*(4), 589–600. http://dx.doi.org/10.1108/00907321211277387.

Massis, B. E. (2012). Librarians and faculty collaboration—partners in student success. *New Library World, 113*(1/2), 90–93. http://dx.doi.org/10.1108/03074801211199077.

Meulemans, Y. N., & Carr, A. (2013). Not at your service: building genuine faculty-librarian partnerships. *Reference Services Review, 41*(1), 80–90. http://dx.doi.org/10.1108/00907321311300893.

Oakleaf, M., Hoover, S., Woodard, B., Corbin, J., Hensley, R., Wakimoto, D., et al. (2012). Notes from the field. *Communications in Information Literacy, 6*(1), 5–23.

Ostrow, M. (2010). Faculty-librarian collaborations at the University of Texas: curricular collaboration—information literacy and the core freshmen curriculum. *Texas Library Journal, 86*(4), 138–139.

Øvern, K. M. (2014). Faculty-library collaboration: two pedagogical approaches. *Journal of Information Literacy, 8*(2), 36–55. http://dx.doi.org/10.11645/8.2.1910.

Pan, D., Ferrer-Vinent, I. J., & Bruehl, M. (2014). Library value in the classroom: assessing student learning outcomes from instruction and collections. *The Journal of Academic Librarianship, 40*(3–4), 332–338. http://dx.doi.org/10.1016/j.acalib.2014.04.011.

Reeves, L., Nishimuta, C., McMillan, J., & Godin, C. (2003). Faculty outreach a win-win proposition. *Reference Librarian, 39*(82), 57–68. http://dx.doi.org/10.1300/J120v39n82_05.

Reynolds, L. M., Smith, S. E., & D'Silva, M. U. (2013). The search for elusive social media data: an evolving librarian–faculty collaboration. *The Journal of Academic Librarianship, 39*(5), 378–384. http://dx.doi.org/10.1016/j.acalib.2013.02.007.

Ringle, M. (2014). Redesigning library instruction: a collaborative process. *Indiana Libraries, 33*(2), 68–70.

Rockman, I. F. (2002). Strengthening connections between information literacy, general education, and assessment efforts. *Library Trends, 51*, 185–261.

Rugan, E. G., & Nero, M. D. (2013). Library scavenger hunts: the good, the bad, and the ugly. *Southeastern Librarian, 61*(3), 7–10.

Sanborn, L. (2005). Perspectives on…improving library instruction: faculty collaboration. *The Journal of Academic Librarianship, 31*(5), 477–481. http://dx.doi.org/10.1016/j.acalib.2005.05.010.

Shane, J. M. Y. (2004). Formal and informal structures for collaboration on a campus-wide information literacy program. *Resource Sharing and Information Networks, 17*(1/2), 85–110.

Simons, A. (2009). Librarians and faculty working together at the University of Houston. *Texas Library Journal, 85*(4), 126–128.

Stebelman, S., Siggins, J. A., & Nutty, D. J. (1999). Improving library relations with the faculty and university administrators: the role of the faculty outreach librarian at George Washington University. *College and Research Libraries, 60*(2), 121–130.

Stein, L. L., & Lamb, J. M. (1998). Not just another BI: faculty-librarian collaboration to guide students through the research process. *Research Strategies*, *16*(1), 29–39. http://dx.doi.org/10.1016/S0734-3310(98)90004-0.

Tillman, C. (2008). Library orientation for professors: give a pitch, not a tour. *College and Research Libraries News*, *69*(8), 470–475.

Victor, P., Jr., Otto, J., & Mutschler, C. (2013). Assessment of library instruction on undergraduate student success in a documents-based research course: the benefits of librarian, archivist, and faculty collaboration. *Collaborative Librarianship*, *5*(3), 154–176.

Virtue, A., & Esparza, L. (2013). Faculty reconnect. *College and Research Libraries News*, *74*(2), 80–99.

Watson, S. E., Rex, C., Markgraf, J., Jennings, E., Kishel, H., & Hinnant, K. (2013). Revising the "one-shot" through lesson study: collaborating with writing faculty to rebuild a library instruction session. *College and Research Libraries*, *74*(4), 381–398.

Wijayasundara, N. D. (2008). Faculty–library collaboration: a model for University of Colombo. *The International Information and Library Review*, *40*(3), 188–198. http://dx.doi.org/10.1080/10572317.2008.10762781.

Zhang, W. (2001). Building partnerships in liberal arts education: library team teaching. *Reference Services Review*, *29*(2), 141–149.

CHAPTER 4

Assessing Classroom Dynamics

4.1 PREPARING FOR ONE-SHOT INSTRUCTION SESSIONS

When planning for instruction sessions, librarians have a tendency to focus all of their attention on the content to be presented. This is usually because there is a great amount of content to share with students and unfortunately not much time to do so. However, there is a danger of depersonalization, in which students become little more than a faceless crowd to the instruction librarian. To avoid this, librarians should attempt to determine the characteristics of the students who will make up their audience. Yet, the basic goals of library instruction should remain the same, that is, for students to learn how to navigate the library's resources and select the best materials for their research. The subject matter of the course and the students' assignments will also inform their research needs (Willis & Thomas, 2006).

When planning an instruction session, instructors should try to answer questions related to the desired learning outcomes, what students should learn, and how to get students to that point (Finley, Skarl, Cox, & VanderPol, 2005). When choosing a topic to demonstrate the use of library tools, the IL instructor should think of one that is relevant to their audience. Usually, current events and real-life examples will capture and hold the attention of an audience (Byrne, 2014). Yet, the makeup of the audience can also be used to guide the planning and delivery style of instruction. In determining the learning objectives for an IL session, instruction librarians should think about how they can most effectively teach students with varied characteristics. A good way to decide on delivery style is to discuss the group's learning preferences with the faculty member beforehand. To choose a delivery style, IL instructors should know who their audience is, which includes more than their age, ethnicity, and gender. Preparing

The Fortuitous Teacher
ISBN 978-0-08-100193-6

an instruction session with this in mind will most likely increase the effectiveness of the instruction. However, regardless of the final delivery style and activities chosen, the basic goals of library instruction should remain the same (Willis & Thomas, 2006).

Instruction librarians are also encouraged to pay attention to other professions, such as stand-up comedy, when choosing a delivery style. Considered masters at appraising their audience, comedians have the ability to spontaneously change their delivery style during a routine. They are experts at relating to people on a personal level and are known to continually revise their material as necessary. Instruction librarians will find that the underlying performance methods used by comedians can easily be applied, and may be beneficial to library instruction presentations (Tewell, 2014). Along with a bit of spontaneity, a little planned humor will help to support the points being made during a presentation. Those instructors who have doubts about their ability to spontaneously deliver jokes can still add life to IL presentations with a little preplanning. Software such as Microsoft PowerPoint is a great tool for adding humor to a lecture by inserting humorous photographs, graphics, cartoons, and even audio files to lighten up the mood and enhance the content. Although search examples should remain relevant to the audience, they can also be humorous or unusual. IL librarians should consider moving beyond standard overused search terms and replace them with interesting, current, and unusual topics (Trefts & Blakeslee, 2000).

The theater world is another arena that instruction librarians can look to for presentation tips. A basic but vital practice in the theater world is the all-important rehearsal. Rehearsing a presentation increases the presenter's confidence and allows for a refinement of the material before meeting the audience. Rehearsing also prepares the instructor for any surprises, in that knowing the material very well usually helps to deal with any unexpected events during the presentation. Videotaping a rehearsal is a great way to assess your presentation, to see what needs improvement, and make any necessary changes beforehand. Asking trusted colleagues to view your presentation and provide positive feedback is another good way to assess the presentation (Antonelli, Kempe, & Sidberry, 2000). This type of self-reflection and feedback from colleagues allows the instruction librarian to have time to productively reflect on their presentation. They should use that time to determine what went well and what needs to be changed and improved upon for the actual presentation (Gewirtz, 2012).

Some librarians even perform database searches ahead of time to be sure that the search will produce the desired results for the demonstration portion of the session. It is also important to develop an organized presentation and to be prepared with the relevant handouts and materials needed to conduct the class. Dressing in a professional manner, being organized, and practicing the presentation are all ways to ensure being and feeling prepared to present. Prior to the start of the session, it is a good idea to arrive early enough to make sure that all of the equipment works, and that there are no problems with Internet connectivity (Oswald & Turnage, 2000). For those instructors who plan to use technology such as clickers during the session, it is a good idea to do a test run and practice using the technology beforehand. Testing the technology with colleagues at a meeting is a great way to do this, using sample questions. This initial testing of the equipment is critical because it allows the instructor to gauge not only the effectiveness of the technology but factors such as average response time. It gives instructors enough time to address any issues that may crop up. Once it is determined that the technology operates successful, it can then be incorporated into instruction sessions (Hoffman & Goodwin, 2006).

Not only can IL librarians test out technology with colleagues, but they can learn from the experiences of other instruction librarians. Some librarians state that their most frequent resource of information and guidance about instruction comes from their colleagues (Sinkinson & Alexander, 2008). Yet many librarians plan and prepare for classes independently, with little input from colleagues. To avoid this, some libraries create peer-coaching teams of instruction librarians with the goal of improving IL instruction, especially for the planning phase. Instruction teams can meet as a group to brainstorm new teaching techniques or ways to modify their classes. The structured use of peer-coaching teams during the planning stages of the one-shot session helps to offset classroom isolation and builds supportive partnerships.

Peer coaching allows IL librarians to receive feedback on their strengths and weaknesses, improve their classroom presentations, learn more about the library system, and feel more like a team (Finley et al., 2005).

Some libraries use structured lesson plans as a foundation for any librarian to build on and develop their own teaching style. This includes packets of materials, such as handouts and exercises kept in stock so that instructors can quickly prepare for a class. All of the IL sessions are of the same length, with each segment of the lesson being a specific period. Each segment consists of teaching points and exercises to keep instructors focused and guided by the time constraints (Houlson, 2007).

Simply assessing a class session is another strategy that can be used to discover which areas of the lesson might need more attention when preparing for future sessions, especially those sessions in which the same material is taught to different groups of students. Even just reviewing results from class quizzes can help decide which content to cover in future classes, giving more attention to subject matter in which the students performed the weakest (Lê, 2012).

Instruction librarians should also plan for sessions by thinking about what students will actually need to know by the end of an IL session to be successful in a particular class or point in their higher-education career. After narrowing the lesson plan to its essentials, the next step may be to decide what to do in class and what to do outside of class. Consider which of the learning outcomes and content require hands-on practice or discussion and interaction for students to achieve some level of understanding. These types of outcomes can be well aligned to active-learning strategies and so are great candidates to remain on the in-class plan. Determine which content or instruction can be moved out of class to create space for active learning and engagement. As well, students should be encouraged to prepare before class by reviewing content and to follow up with any questions after class.

Lesson plans for IL sessions should include the learning outcomes, a teaching strategy focused on student learning, and some type of assessment of the learning. The plan should estimate the amount of time each activity will take, especially when incorporating a new activity. A good goal may be to keep lecturing to a minimum and to focus on student-centered activity instead. Tracking the time for each element of the lesson plan helps to determine how many learning outcomes can actually fit into the available time. Asking a colleague to observe the lesson while timing each section can be useful to determine this. Including details about what students should learn from each outcome and how to know that they have learned them may also be beneficial. Evidence of learning can be as simple as students accurately completing a worksheet or correctly answering a series of questions. In this way, the assessment is built into the activity. Other helpful tips are having a list of examples to show during a demonstration or a note to oneself to make sure students understand the directions provided for an activity they will complete. After the session, make a note of what worked, what did not, what to remember for the next session, and anything else that may help to improve student learning. Using the same lesson planning approach and format between colleagues is a great time-saver in that information can be shared, and they can learn from each other. This can even include a list of materials needed during the session, such as pens, specific handouts, sign-in sheets, and technology (Oakleaf et al., 2012).

The Coordinator of Library Instruction at the Emerson College Library led a retreat with the teaching team to solicit criticism, define goals, and devise strategies for improving the experiences of members of the teaching team. Before the retreat, the librarians were asked to focus less on the tools that they thought students needed to use and more on IL concepts. Instead of following a prepared script, they tailored sessions to respond to student needs in the research process. They worked with professors to design assignments and sessions that would help students to understand information resources, determine information needs, find and evaluate information, and effectively use information. Working with faculty allowed them to share teaching tips, techniques, and activities. The instruction librarians inevitably found that preparing for classes under the new model was time consuming because they no longer relied on scripts and outlines but spent more time working with faculty members and researching to prepare for a class. However, this move toward a model of partnering with faculty did not mean that they gave up the responsibility of designing content for library sessions. Instead, they moved forward to build a model in which both the faculty members and the librarians were able to define learning outcomes for sessions together (Litten, 2002).

4.2 PENETRATING THE ACADEMIC CLASSROOM CULTURE

Partnering with faculty to prepare for IL sessions goes beyond the content of a lesson plan. Librarians should enlist the help of the classroom instructor to emphasize the importance of the upcoming session and to ask that the students give the librarian the respect and attention they would give any visitor to their class (Vander Meer, Ring, & Perez-Stable, 2007).

During one-shot sessions, librarians are tasked with presenting information to a group of students who have already established an order of interaction, a culture of sorts. To quickly penetrate that culture so that the attention of the students is gained and maintained in a very short time, start out by welcoming the students, which helps to establish a rapport and build relationships with even the most challenging students. Arriving to the classroom early demonstrates that their presence is valued and sets a friendly tone for the session. To prevent potential distractions, try to circulate around the room, and communicate with the students sitting in the back. Overall, this provides those with questions greater opportunities to be heard. Individually, students will feel that they are being heard if the authoritarian nature of the interaction is removed. An authoritarian tone can impede the teacher's efforts to work with a student. An easy way to overcome this and build collegiality is to sit next to the student or squat, instead of leaning over and talking down to them. Moreover, of course, the common courtesy of using words such as please and thank you creates an atmosphere of mutual respect and friendliness (Scripps-Hoekstra, 2013).

Before the start of the session, as the students begin to arrive, be sure to make contact with them. Start by passing any class materials, maintaining a calm and confident demeanor, even if you do not feel it, and try to make small talk. At the start of the session, remember to introduce yourself to the students, even if their instructor has already introduced you. Make mention of what you do, and why you are there. Give the students an informal overview of what will be covered and what they can expect during the session (Oswald & Turnage, 2000).

Deemer (2007) discusses the use of a preclass presentation with music and graphics designed to grab the students' attention as they enter the room. The looping slides contain humorous pictures and provide information about the library in the form of multiple-choice questions. The librarian can encourage students to try to answer the questions as they settle in and wait for class to begin. The slide presentation also defines library and research terms which may be unfamiliar to students and creates a common vocabulary from which to refer and build upon during the session. Students seem to enjoy the preclass presentation, and it is a great way to get the class off to a positive start.

The first 5 min are often deemed the most important of any time instructors (whether they are librarians or professors) spend with their class. In addition to setting the tone of the presentation and breaking the ice, the instructor must use this time to create a connection with the students, get them invested in the content, and challenge them to think critically. The main goal of the anticipatory set is to grab the students' attention and hook them into the class. It provides an important preview of the class content and learning objectives. In addition to setting the tone, the anticipatory set provides an opportunity to create a connection with students and challenge them to think (Deemer, 2007).

A popular icebreaker activity called "Question Posting" involves the instructor asking students to spend a minute writing down the concerns, issues, or expectations they have regarding the class. The instructor then collects the questions and records these concerns and ideas for the class to see. This method of writing down and sharing questions helps both the teacher and the students to become better acquainted with each other, and introduce active participation to the classroom. The premise is that through this activity an interactive give-and-take tone is established between student and instructor (Hanz & Lange, 2013).

To effectively penetrate the culture of a class during an IL session, some librarians simply engage their students in conversation about how they view and use information. This simple strategy allows a give and take between student and librarian, who can gain an understanding of who the students are without conducting a formal study. It is possible to learn directly from the students about who they are, what their needs are, as well as their online habits, such as what they do online and how much time they spend doing it (Jacobs, 2008). This type of dialog is a great motivation to get students involved in the learning process. Asking students about their love of the library, whether they have had a tour of the building, or simply about their current assignment is a great place to start (Oswald & Turnage, 2000).

Librarians can also incorporate active-learning exercises, which also help to capture student interest. Specifically, exercise sheets add variety to the typical monotony of listening to a traditional lecture. Worksheets also create built-in time for students to work on their current research assignments, which is important, because students have been found to be more receptive to learning library research skills if the skills are relevant to their immediate academic needs. They also tend to retain the information if they use it immediately. Another technique which can be used to infiltrate this culture is to circulate around the class, immediately addressing questions and problems that may arise during the session. In addition, stopping to ask questions can encourage students to think, reflect, apply, and demonstrate the topic at hand (Bladek & Okamoto, 2014).

Even physical exercises can be employed to liven up IL sessions. These can range from interactive tours of the library involving finding books, to activities such as "Boolean Simon Says," which demonstrates how Boolean operators work by asking the students to stand up if they meet certain criteria. In general, active learning techniques such as these engage students and maintain student interest (Bladek & Okamoto, 2014). Adding games to lesson plans may seem risky; however, students tend to appreciate the thought and effort put into creating an engaging learning experience, whether it goes smoothly or not. Of course, without enthusiasm any lesson, including games or not, will most certainly be less effective. Enthusiasm can be communicated by using a more animated style of voice and gesture. Most importantly, be sure to smile and show passion for the subject matter, which makes a great difference in engaging student attention (Scripps-Hoekstra, 2013).

Games motivate students to actively participate in a class session, especially one-shot library instruction sessions. Some students are stimulated by the competition of certain games because they can choose to more actively participate during the session. Games add variety to classes by providing a fun environment for both instructors and students. Students usually prefer games as a more fun way to review material and often view them as a welcomed break from the usual lecture experience in the classroom (Walker, 2008).

When faced with a large lecture hall of students, many IL librarians quickly realize that to be truly heard they have to develop the ability to be entertaining. Telling jokes is one of the quickest ways to "break the ice" in any classroom setting. In fact, humor helps most people hear and retain information more easily. Starting the session with an icebreaker, anecdote, or personal experience which is relevant to the subject matter encourages ongoing give and take with students (Jacobs, 2008). Online polling tools can be used for icebreaker exercises, for pre- and posttests, and for gathering feedback about instruction sessions (Farkas, 2012). Relaying the subject matter in a personal way is another way to effectively engage students. Librarians usually find that they must achieve the perfect balance between the roles of entertainer and technical and information specialist (Jacobs, 2008). Cultivating humor can be as simple as smiling or coming across in a light-hearted, spontaneous, and natural manner. A loose, conversational attitude lends itself to an informal atmosphere. In addition, paying close attention to student comments during a session is also important as they can be used to build student involvement (Walker, 2006).

At Brigham Young University Library (BYU) a project was undertaken to modify one of four existing classrooms to provide a room that could adapt to various teaching and learning needs to reenergize teaching and learning at the BYU library. The expected outcome of the changes was that student learning would improve, and teachers would experience increased energy and enthusiasm in relation to their instruction sessions by integrating creative teaching approaches to the content. This study showed that changing the classroom environment for IL instruction can have a positive impact on teacher and student behavior. By changing the seating in one classroom from fixed to moveable furniture and providing students with iPads, the routine was disrupted. The librarians adapted to this disruption by experimenting with their lesson plans and incorporating more interactive activities. They were vital to the success of the classroom redesign and being provided with the time to adapt to the new classroom created new energy in the library instruction program, which most likely increased student satisfaction with their IL instruction (Julian, 2013).

The conversational technique of using "Yes, and…" promotes participation from the entire class. By accepting everyone's input and not ignoring anything, an egalitarian environment of communication is created. The students are encouraged not to censor themselves, which allows comments of all kinds into the conversation. Off-topic comments or even heckling can be beneficial to the entire class if the exchange is routed in a positive direction. Each and every interaction with a student should be taken seriously. The person speaking should have the instructor's full attention and their comment viewed as a valuable addition to the lesson. Librarians are encouraged to simply be honest, focused, and enthusiastic in their responses instead of making an effort to be funny or clever. The more relaxed and quick thinking they are, the more naturally clever responses will come during presentations. Undoubtedly, natural talent plays a big factor; however, ad-libbing skills can be developed. This involves the ability to see humor in others' comments as much or more than being able to make funny comments yourself; having a high degree of awareness of the audience's mood, which can change rapidly, and sensitivity to the audience's attitudes, especially to what could be interpreted as offensive. The inability to gauge the audience in this way can result in the class becoming unproductive, unresponsive, and unsuccessful (Vossler & Sheidlower, 2001).

4.3 SHOWTIME: SETTING THE TONE

Attempting to set the tone at the start of a class is a well-known pedagogical technique. By setting the tone, the instructor gives students cues for expectations, attitudes, motivation, behavior, and learning.

Displaying great enthusiasm for the subject can be enough to carry the students along with the instructor in the first 5 min of the session. Inevitably, the students pick up on that enthusiasm and are automatically more willing to listen and better able to retain what is being said. This helps to break the ice, making it much easier to begin the presentation on a positive note (Oswald & Turnage, 2000). Along with enthusiasm, showing commitment to the topic and displaying some personality contribute to student engagement. Enthusiasm, reciprocal in nature, prompts students to interact with the instructor and the content. Its authentic and naturally humanizing quality serves to intensify the message being relayed (Oakleaf et al., 2012).

Some librarians find that the theatrical element of teaching allows them to express an amplified version of themselves. Just like actors, teachers address a group made up of individuals. Moreover, like any good performer, those who teach must be able to reach the whole audience, but can only do this by reaching the individuals that make up that audience (Oakleaf et al., 2012). However, there is a big difference between a good performer and a good teacher. Good teachers focus on teaching, rather than performing. They move around the classroom, interacting with students, taking the focus off of them and placing it back on the students. Good teachers try to always be aware of student responses so that they can easily gauge how many individuals grasp what is being taught and modify activities accordingly, which increases motivation (Alsop & Bergart, 2007).

Yet, good teachers are not only aware of their audience but of themselves as well. It is a good idea to not stand behind the podium, being sure to move around, even going up and down aisles if possible. Of course, be aware of the surroundings, being careful not to trip over wires, bags, or fall down stairs in a lecture hall. Lively mannerisms and maintaining good eye contact are also great ways to hold on to the attention of students, especially those sitting in the back and on the sides (Vander Meer et al., 2007).

Developing vibrant and expressive speech patterns is also important. Recording oneself speaking can be useful to analyze the tone, pattern, and rhythm of your speech. Through regular daily practice, certain aspects of speech such as rhythm, melody, pitch, and pause allows for the development of new speaking habits. To that end, simply reading out loud from a book for 20 or 30 min once or twice a day can be especially useful. Make a point to be expressive, with appropriate emotion, and vary the pitch, tone, and pace depending on the text. Not only does this practice help to develop good habits of expression, but it also helps to strengthen the voice. Ultimately, exercising the voice to improve speaking skills sets the tone of the performance and results in teaching that is more effective (Schoofs, 2010).

As far as the audience, those who are auditory learners prefer to learn through listening. They are especially receptive to auditory stimuli that involve varied tone, rhythm, and pitch. General recommendations for providing aural stimulation in the classroom usually involve the use of music as a memorization device (for example, singing the alphabet) or playing background music to enhance the general learning environment. The regular incorporation of music in IL sessions is an excellent way to add interest and variety to IL instruction (Kimball & O'Conner, 2010).

The use of humor in teaching is a technique that can be effective regardless of the size of the class. Telling jokes, funny stories, or even using different accents (depending on the subject matter) are all great techniques to put students at ease. For example, when talking about the features of Library of Congress subject headings, point out humorous headings such as "military miniatures" which describes what are commonly referred to as "toy soldiers." Alternatively, when discussing web research showing the students amusing fake websites will stress the point that they need to critically evaluate the web sources that they use in their research. Humor should improve communication and motivate students. Above all, it should reflect the speaker and should never exclude anyone in the classroom (Vander Meer et al., 2007). Just as timing is a huge part of successfully delivering humor on stage, so it is as well when conducting a class session. Consider that some of the material may need to be left out to save time. Also, maybe include fewer search demonstrations and instead spend more time teaching research concepts. Especially in a large group setting, keep time limitations and pacing in mind because any instruction other than a lecture may take even more time. Think about dividing the elements of the session into segments, for instance, including visual media or an activity to provide variety (Vander Meer et al., 2007).

On the one hand, using interactive exercises to foster student participation is vital. However, on the other hand incorporating silence and reflection during instruction sessions can increase comprehension. Because many students lead busy and stressful lives, silence can often relieve that stress. Likewise, it can sometimes improve the general classroom climate (Alsop & Bergart, 2007).

In general, setting a positive tone is important and becomes even more so when teaching a large group of students, which can easily dissolve into lethargy and indifference. Students who might otherwise be attentive may view themselves as exempt from the instructor's observation, and may feel that they are simply part of an anonymous mass. The librarian should communicate expectations at the beginning of the class, letting the students know that the information being taught is valuable, will save them time, and possibly earn them a better grade. It also helps to suggest that if students have a question they should raise their hand instead of asking their neighbor (Vander Meer et al., 2007).

Another popular technique for working with large groups is querying the students and requiring that they raise their hands in answer. This technique allows all of the students to take some action during the session. Asking specific rather than broad questions is best, for example, instead of simply asking students if they have questions try asking them if there are specific points that they would like to be repeated or clarified (Vander Meer et al., 2007). Constant feedback on session progress is motivating and keeps students on track. Another motivator is incorporating simple wellness strategies such as stretch breaks and contemplation, which can help to create an atmosphere more conducive to learning (Alsop & Bergart, 2007).

Alternatively, tools like Poll Everywhere, an online polling system, allow everyone to participate and help to keep students interested in the presentation. Not only do students and faculty find it beneficial to their learning, but everyone has fun using it (Gewirtz, 2012). Generally, students respond very positively to web-based polling during library instruction sessions, and it also helps to hold their attention (Hoppenfeld, 2012). Anonymous response systems like Wiffiti can build the confidence of students who feel uncomfortable speaking in public, and allow them to share their ideas and ask questions discreetly (Farkas, 2012).

Good communication and positive remarks also keep students focused and energized. Students can sense if an instructor is truly engaged with the class or simply going through the motions. If a class is more about the instructor's own performance rather than student learning, or the instructor rarely moves from the center of the stage, students can lose motivation or tune out altogether. Although it may be difficult, to establish a rapport with students that you may interact with only once, try leaving the security of the front of the class. This movement is encouraging to the students because they feel that the instructor is more in tune with the class (Alsop & Bergart, 2007).

Another factor to consider is the demographics of the audience, for example, their general age. Knowing who the audience is can have an impact on creating a positive tone. Instruction librarians should also understand and accommodate the physical and psychological needs of their audience. The goal is to create a program that will be effective for the greatest number of people. Remember that the audience will be physically and psychologically distressed if they are forced to sit still in uncomfortable chairs and listen to a lecturer drone on for hours on end. Be very careful that all library assignments, and all content covered in the session, are nondiscriminatory. Keep in mind that the use of jargon could be confusing to nonnative speakers, and certain types of cultural, religious, or political examples might be offensive to some (Saunders, 2002). For many adult and senior learners returning to the classroom, the experience of using the library in today's fast-paced technological environment can be a daunting and challenging experience. Many return to the college classroom with more anxiety, fear, and uncertainty about using computer technology and searching the Internet than traditional students (Gust, 2006).

4.4 STRATEGIES FOR ENGAGING STUDENT INTEREST

Active learning, a student–centered instruction method, is considered a key strategy for engaging student interest and participation through activities such as group discussion, investigation, experimentation, and role play. At MacEwan University Library, a training manual was developed to guide preparation for instruction sessions and outline a collection of active-learning activities. Although this meant more time preparing for sessions beforehand, it was rewarded by increased student and librarian engagement during sessions. Students appeared to be much more engaged and interested when the active-learning activities were employed. The activity called Press Conference Cards allows students to ask and respond to questions about using library services. The Synonym Race is a timed activity which encourages students to think of keyword alternatives. To demonstrate Boolean logic the activity called Shuffle and Deal asks students to stand according to the card they have received. Moreover, Scrimmage allows students to choose how they want to research a specific topic to facilitate a discussion about the most effective research strategies (Shamchuk & Plouffe, 2013).

Other factors to consider for engaging students are the arrangement of the physical space, implementing a course theme, conducting discussions, and incorporating reflective writing exercises. The physical layout of the room has an especially positive impact on the interaction level of the students. Librarians should consider teaching in classrooms with moveable tables, chairs, and laptops. Students are able to sit at tables in groups of three or four, which makes it easier for them to work together on group activities (Mayer & Bowles-Terry, 2013).

Similar to movable laptops, the use of iPads in library instruction produces a high level of student engagement, making hands-on instruction worth the risk, time, and effort. Students benefit more from guided practice and interaction with their peers, rather than listening passively to an instructor. The use of iPads makes it possible to engage students for longer periods. Because the devices provide each student with a digital portal to online and library resources, they can easily experiment with employing various search strategies. Many libraries are using tablets for reference and circulation; however, iPads for instructional use should be considered as they can facilitate a transition toward inquiry-based learning (Sullivan, 2014).

Music also has a high impact on student engagement in the classroom. In 2010, librarians at Western Michigan University investigated the effect of background music on student engagement and retention of IL concepts. Results from that study indicate positive correlations between background music and student comfort, confidence, and retention. The study also suggests that background music is an effective tool in promoting student satisfaction and learning. Allowing students to vote on the type of music played can also be an opportunity to increase student engagement and involvement in the development of the classroom environment. The majority of students in the study enjoyed the use of the background music and showed improved retention of IL concepts. This pilot study used participants from typical "one-shot" IL classes. It is possible that the impact of background music on students is greater in the "one-shot" environment than in traditional semester-long courses. This is because students are in an unfamiliar and temporary environment, different from their regular "home" classroom, and may experience greater levels of discomfort and intimidation. Background music can be used as a tool to help students to relax and to improve the classroom atmosphere in general (Langan & Sachs, 2013). Just like music, video is also a great medium for increasing student engagement during library instruction. This applies to all age groups, not just younger students. It is recommended that librarians watch other librarians' videos for presentation tips, such as keeping them animated yet informative, and making sure the videos are lively and fast-paced (Ojala, 2013).

As a former high school history teacher, Lindy Scripps-Hoekstra (2013) spent 3 years "in the trenches" developing methods to design effective and engaging learning experiences. She shares strategies that transfer very well to higher education IL instruction sessions, such as getting to the classroom early so that you can welcome your students by greeting them warmly and setting a friendly tone for the session. She also suggests moving around the classroom, which can prevent misbehavior and hold the attention of the students at the back of the room. Maintaining an atmosphere of mutual respect is important, along with letting students know that session activities are not optional. Phrasing directives in this way encourages all students to follow along. Most importantly, make an effort to show enthusiasm through lively voice and gesture, which makes it easier to engage students, along with smiling and showing passion for the subject matter.

In searching for ways to make the classroom experience more engaging some instructors have turned to audience response systems, such as clickers or web-polling applications (Walker & Pearce, 2014). Lasers can have a similar effect. Using laser pointers serves the purpose of keeping students engaged and focused on what they are learning. Another aspect of using the pointers is that they tend to make the class more entertaining; the novelty of the lasers alone provides a bit of fun and initial engagement with the session (Zdravkovska, Cech, Beygo, & Kackley, 2010).

Another strategy for engaging student interest involves adding popular culture examples to in-class assignments. This taps into student emotion, evoking strong reactions in students, and these emotions allow deeper learning to occur. If the appropriate example is chosen, students will enthusiastically engage in library instruction sessions. The students should have a prior interest, or at the very least, a high comfort level with the topic, allowing the instructor to focus on what they already know and build on more complex information. Regardless of the popular culture topic employed, being willing to try different teaching methods is crucial for the use of popular culture in IL instruction. When trying unusual ideas, there is an even greater need for hands-on exercises in which the students can apply IL skills. Application of these skills is also important when proving effectiveness to faculty members, who may have reservations about incorporating popular culture references. Instruction librarians have many options for staying current with popular culture, such as library student employees and library subscriptions to popular magazines such as Entertainment Weekly and People Magazine, which feature popular television shows and celebrity gossip (Springer & Yelinek, 2011).

Strategies to increase student engagement can also be applied to online IL sessions. Online students should be provided with a forum to share their experiences, thoughts, and interests. If the instructor makes an effort to repeat their contribution back to the group, it will confirm the value of their participation and encourage them to do so going forward. Likewise, giving individual students specific responsibilities in the online classroom encourages participation. This can be achieved by having individual students post questions about the research process, and then asking all students to respond to those questions. Similarly, students can advise each other about their assignments, and this advice can then be made available on a libguide or web page for future students. Other online tools, such as Poll Everywhere, Instagram, and Twitter hashtags, can be used to gather student responses during an online instruction session, which increases interactivity and results in greater student engagement (Cuthbertson & Falcone, 2014).

There are many options for keeping an online class both interesting and interactive for students. The three main areas to keep in mind are use of technology, content creation methods, and communication or interaction with the class. Instruction librarians should keep informed about what technology is available, how to use that technology, and how to create content within that medium. Effective communication is vital and involves both student interaction and student/instructor interaction. Interaction between all parties allows for a richer learning environment in which everyone feels more involved and invested in the class (Farwell, 2013).

4.5 PARTNERING WITH FACULTY DURING INSTRUCTION SESSIONS

In 2001, Zhang stated that if the new academic library is to become a teaching library, then it is imperative for librarians to build partnerships with teaching faculty of the institution and get closely involved in curricular development. Bibliographic instruction is a primary means for librarians to develop close relationships with classroom teachers. To this end, the Rollins College Olin Library and History Department worked closely to design and teach a for-credit course titled, "Library Research: America and England in the Eighteenth Century." The Olin reference librarians found working with classroom faculty to design and teach a library course to be very challenging and rewarding at the same time. Without a formal background in pedagogy, understanding and applying advanced learning theories to classroom teaching proved to be a difficult task for the librarians involved. However, partnering with classroom teachers provided instruction librarians with an excellent opportunity to learn from experienced faculty. They became better teachers and consequently were able to provide better instructional services to students. Team teaching requires the highest level of collaborative work between librarians and departmental faculty. Although it can be time consuming and labor intensive, especially at the early stages of course development, the benefits of being able to share ideas and support each other are substantial. Team teaching not only reduces librarians' isolation and increases their sense of accomplishment, but it also provides a strong foundation for librarians to develop long-term partnerships with classroom faculty in promoting IL skills to the campus academic community (Zhang, 2001).

On the one hand, long-term partnerships with faculty who are enthusiastic and knowledgeable about IL can produce assignments that encourage students to use library resources both creatively and systematically. On the other hand, if a faculty member incorporates IL with a feeling of obligation but no real understanding of its value, students will quickly sense this attitude and view the IL session as unimportant. Even when the librarian is welcomed into the class, there is seldom any chance to participate in determining the nature of the assignment itself. The instruction librarian is involved in neither the preparation nor the evaluation of the final product. The absence of involvement and authority is not lost on students (Carlson & Miller, 1984).

However, if the faculty member is actively involved during library sessions by answering students' content-specific questions, the importance of the librarian's instruction is reinforced. Close collaboration between librarians and faculty during IL sessions produces a solid learning environment in which the subject content blends seamlessly with the required research and evaluation skills (Black, Crest, & Volland, 2001).

Faculty behavior during IL sessions can be a concern, for example, grading papers or reading while librarians are teaching or even going away to conferences when sessions are scheduled. Faculty members have been characterized as being irresponsible, having bad manners, constantly interrupting, making comments, or correcting the librarian during instructional sessions. Instruction librarians can remedy these concerns by referring to the professor during the session so that students view the librarian and professor as a united front (Given & Julien, 2003).

Faculty members should be encouraged to be present at the IL session, which will encourage more of their students to attend and benefit from the session. Students understand that they are accountable to their instructor, and not to the librarian, for their course grade. Faculty can be asked to provide the course-related context to a principle or skill covered by the librarian. This type of collaboration and the presence of the instructor will help to validate the importance of IL instruction. Conversely, the absence of the instructor can send the opposite message (Ellison, 2004).

These considerations apply to online courses as well. In fall 2001, two Austin Peay State University (APSU) librarians partnered with a communications professor to develop and teach an online graduate course in communications topics entitled Multimedia Literacy. At the time, the development and team teaching of online courses by librarians and faculty was a new type of partnership. The goal of the librarians was to help remote access students to develop IL skills. By collaborating with the instructors they developed web-based assignments that helped distance students to master basic IL competencies. Collaborating more directly with faculty ensures that IL is integrated to the greatest degree possible with course content. Team teaching a course with classroom faculty provides librarians with an exciting opportunity to truly integrate IL into the students' education. The librarian and teaching faculty are able to build trust in each other's expertise and experience, which paves the way for the smooth coordination of duties. The librarians relied upon the communications professor for subject expertise, for example, on what information the students should already know from other classes in the degree program, and for guidance in handling the classroom management duties with which librarians were unfamiliar (Buchanan, Luck, & Jones, 2002). Dividing responsibilities in this way best utilizes individual instructor strengths and interests. For those sessions which the librarian does not lead, they can be active participants and assistants, as well allowing for the evaluation of students' overall progress (Ricker, 1998).

Matching strengths and personalities to responsibilities is an important component of successful team teaching, especially when the librarian's role is incorporated into the class to a high degree. In preparing for the session, both librarian and instructor can share equally in the organization, active presentation role, and evaluation of the class. However, personality conflicts and differences in instructional style and philosophy can make team teaching an unpleasant and unproductive experience. The members of any team must be willing to give up some control and ego, which team teaching requires. It can be a threatening proposition for a faculty member to invite an outside instructor to share control of his or her classroom (Isbell & Broaddus, 1995).

To avoid this, the team-teaching approach should start with a meeting between teacher and librarian in which learning objectives and assignments are discussed. This meeting is vital as it lays the foundation for the collaboration. It is important that both librarian and teacher claim ownership of the session and believe in its objectives, as well as the instruction methods used. Both should decide on a plan for the instruction activities, for example, in which one of them will cover specific topics. After the session is conducted, they should collaborate to assess and plan future sessions. Team teaching can be executed as a single-session strategy, part of a course, or whole semester. Although this approach can be used on all class sizes, the nature of the course and the needs of the students should be considered. In the team-teaching approach, the equality of the teacher and the librarian is essential. They must be seen as equals to gain the students' respect (Øvern, 2014).

Along with collaborating to assess instruction sessions, librarians and faculty can conduct phenomenological self-study research to explore their beliefs about and improve the quality of their future collaborations. Positive collaborations will be highly valued by those involved, which will lead to subsequent collaboration. Future collaboration can be expanded to teaching at different academic levels, coauthoring, or even research studies. In general, collaborative instruction can lead to the development of classroom activities that are more comprehensive, complex, creative, and innovative than learning activities developed by individuals working in isolation (Brown & Duke, 2005).

4.6 DEVELOPING CLASSROOM MANAGEMENT SKILLS

Unfortunately, classroom management skills are not taught in library school, and consequently many librarians are forced to learn how to manage a classroom while on the job. Different classroom settings, such as one-shot instruction sessions or for-credit courses, require different management techniques. Techniques will also vary according to the preference and comfort level of the instruction librarian. The need to learn classroom management strategies must be recognized for its importance in successful classes taught by librarians.

Classroom management includes many variables, such as interaction with faculty, student participation, questions, challenges, reactions, unforeseen outcomes, and potentially uncomfortable scenarios. Be prepared for unforeseen situations; however, keep in mind that even overpreparation cannot equip you for every situation. In IL sessions, decisions regarding the governing of the classroom are ultimately the responsibility of the librarian. Developing the skills to manage a classroom is necessary for librarians to conduct successful instruction sessions (Blackburn & Hays, 2014).

Classroom management involves proactively coordinating a class to limit misbehavior and to create stress-free library instruction. Classroom management should be distinguished from discipline, which is the action taken when intervention is necessary to maintain a positive classroom experience. Classroom management is the series of steps taken to prevent undesirable behaviors, whereas discipline is the response to misbehavior. Taking steps to manage a classroom will not prevent misbehavior altogether, which is why both classroom management practices and disciplinary measures are essential to maintaining a positive library classroom (Holbrook, 2014).

Instruction librarians should take the time to consider exactly what their role is when a student acts out or behaves badly during an instruction session. Misbehavior does not refer to the student who simply voices an unpopular opinion, but to the student who answers a cell phone, sends a text message, falls asleep, or becomes intentionally disruptive during a class session. Another issue to consider is what to do when the instructor or teaching assistant misbehaves during a library instruction session. Although many institutions and libraries provide codes of conduct and student handbooks, they do not necessarily address all types of bad behavior, nor the delivery of appropriate consequences. Essentially, how these situations are handled usually depends on the personality and preference of the librarian (Jacobs, 2008).

In Sacks' (1996) study on disruptive classroom behaviors, the following were listed as some common disruptive classroom behaviors: text messaging; making noises or openly yawning; slamming doors while leaving the classroom; working on other assignments; being argumentative, disrespectful, and uncooperative; displaying negative body language such as rolling eyes and shifting noisily; monopolizing discussions; asking personal questions; dressing inappropriately; and talking or laughing over the instructor. Some instructors ignore these behaviors because they fear that confronting them will result in student retaliation, escalation of the behavior, negative comments on faculty evaluations, or complaints to authority figures. Others believe that these behaviors are the norm and that no positive outcome can come from addressing them. More often, however, instructors do not know how to handle these situations, what will work to curb them, or what will backfire. So it is important to address disruptive behaviors immediately. Educators have the responsibility to develop rules and strategies to address disruptive behaviors and to teach students proper control and professionalism. Understanding the characteristics of each cohort of students and preparing strategies for addressing the preventing disruptive behaviors will help both novice and expert teachers be more effective (Murphy, 2010).

Along with setting rules, procedures can be established for library instruction sessions, especially in computer lab settings. Procedures tend to minimize misbehavior and keep students on task. They can also teach cooperative social rules, establish positive interdependence, and ensure individual accountability. Assigning each student a role is a proactive way to ensure individual accountability (Chai et al., 2003).

Avoiding discipline problems and creating an environment conducive to learning is paramount, which means it is vital to gauge students' reactions and respond to the class appropriately. Resources used during the session can also contribute to the climate of the classroom, such as audio-visual resources, color images, or an appealing website versus a text-dominated book. The variety of resources used is also important for motivating pupils, which can reduce the potential for students being distracted from the topic or activity at hand. Be sure that any handouts and flyers are professionally produced and treated with care, because if students feel that the instructor does not respect the subject they can lose interest. Poorly produced, unattractive materials lead to demotivation and make class management more difficult (Reading, 2002).

Class Badges (class-badges.com) allows instructors to create custom badges to award to students for completing assigned tasks and projects. Some instructors find that the application is best used on a weekly basis. Rather than giving out awards each day, distributing badges to students for participating in a week- or month-long series of discussions can work well (Byrne, 2014).

In most hands-on IL sessions, students can be busily engaged while interacting with the resources, materials, and each other. Preparing a print handout that outlines the sequence of activities will help to guide student work. Groups should be engaged in a very structured task with clear, precise learning outcomes. Something as basic as online searching presents a classroom management challenge, in that it hinders eye-to-eye interaction. One solution to this is the use of iPads for searching because they remove the visual obstacle of the laptop or monitor screen in a computer lab. The mobility and size of tablets promote collaboration and conversation, eliminating the physical barrier of the computer and allowing participants to arrange themselves in more flexible configurations (Sullivan, 2014).

Although technology does not take the place of true classroom management, it can certainly help. For instance, during lengthier instruction sessions, it is a good idea to give the students short breaks along with timed, hands-on activities. Online countdown timers can help to keep these breaks from stretching on for too long. Many online timers allow you to create, set, and view multiple timers on one screen. Some timers can even be set to music, such as Mission Impossible, The Apprentice, and other countdown themes. Apps such as Too Noisy help students to learn to recognize the appropriate volume for conversations. The app measures the volume in a room and displays a meter indicating whether or not it is too loud. Randomizers can be useful when all hands are raised to participate in an activity. A Random Name Selector is one simple tool for picking names from a list you've created. To use it, type in or copy a list of names and press "go" (Byrne, 2014). However, the use of technology is not appropriate in all instructional settings. Houtman (as cited in Blackburn & Hays, 2014) notes that some instruction librarians prefer to use it only with smaller groups and find that with groups of more than 20 students it can be difficult to pace activities, especially when providing solo instruction or the librarian is less technically inclined. Thus, pacing during instruction sessions is critical. It can be helpful to introduce some sort of question or activity approximately every 10 min by dividing instruction into multiple segments. After presenting each segment, live or via slide show, insert some sort of active-learning exercise in which responses are shared via an overhead projector (Vander Meer et al., 2007). For those larger groups of over 20 students, a good technique for countering lethargy involves having students stand up and walk around the room. A good strategy for employing this technique is to ask student volunteers to use the keyboard at the front of the room to input search strategies or to write keywords on the board. Another strategy is to ask each leader during a group activity to record their comments on the board for discussion. Using poster paper or giant Post-it notes on the walls to record research questions is another great strategy. After recording their group's work, leaders can then move around the room, adding to and commenting on the questions proposed by other groups. Although these strategies are useful for increasing interaction and collaboration for large classes, it can be unmanageable for very large classes of over 50 to 80 students, keeping ease of movement and safety in mind (Vander Meer et al., 2007).

Team teaching or coteaching should be considered as a way to build confidence and provide moral support for instruction librarians who find risk taking and a loss of control in the classroom to be a scary prospect. Many instruction librarians are averse to introducing unpredictable factors within a class session, whereas others are enthusiastic about adding activities that introduce spontaneity. Differences in teaching preferences can be harnessed to take advantage of the strengths of each instructor involved. At the very least, having a colleague assist in the session, by moving around the room to help students and to provide moral support, can provide a great boost to the confidence of any instruction librarian (Vander Meer et al., 2007).

If using humor is a strength, it can certainly be used as a tool in classroom management. However, keep in mind that students sometimes view the deliberate use of humor as a sign of a teacher's intent to control the classroom. If the humor is viewed as being less than open, honest, and spontaneous it can be more destructive to the communicative climate than the absence of humor. Using humor should be considered and incorporated very carefully, rather than assuming that any humor will automatically enhance the classroom environment. In fact, using obviously planned jokes can have the opposite effect on a classroom climate (MacAdam, 1985). Another highly recommended classroom management tool is to always remember not to talk over students. It is best advised to wait until you have 100% quiet and the full attention of the classroom. Although this is easier said than done, once put into practice, it is a most highly effective classroom management tool (School Library Monthly, 2011).

REFERENCES

Alsop, J., & Bergart, R. (2007). Aerobics and library instruction - an unexpected fit. *College & Undergraduate Libraries*, *14*(3), 121–126. http://dx.doi.org/10.1300/J106v14n03_09.

Antonelli, M., Kempe, J., & Sidberry, G. (2000). And now for something completely different…theatrical techniques for library instruction. *Research Strategies*, *17*(2–3), 177–185. http://dx.doi.org/10.1016/S0734-3310(00)00045-8.

Black, C., Crest, S., & Volland, M. (2001). Building a successful information literacy infrastructure on the foundation of librarian–faculty collaboration. *Research Strategies*, *18*(3), 215–225. http://dx.doi.org/10.1016/S0734-3310(02)00085-X.

Blackburn, H., & Hays, L. (2014). Classroom management and the librarian. *Education Libraries*, *37*(1–2), 23–32.

Bladek, M., & Okamoto, K. (2014). What's theory got to do with it? Applying educational theory and research to revamp freshman library workshops. *College & Undergraduate Libraries*, *21*(1), 19–36. http://dx.doi.org/10.1080/10691316.2014.877730.

Brown, J. D., & Duke, T. S. (2005). Librarian and faculty collaborative instruction: a phenomenological self-study. *Research Strategies*, *20*(3), 171–190. http://dx.doi.org/10.1016/j.resstr.2006.05.001.

Buchanan, L. E., Luck, D. L., & Jones, T. C. (2002). Integrating information literacy into the virtual university: a course model. *Library Trends*, *51*(2), 144–166.

Byrne, R. (2014). Classroom management tricks. *School Library Journal, 60*(10), 15.

Carlson, D., & Miller, R. H. (1984). Librarians and teaching faculty: partners in bibliographic instruction. *College & Research Libraries, 45*(6), 483–491. http://dx.doi.org/10.5860/crl_45_06_483.

Chai, C. S., Divaharan, S., Khine, M. S., Lim, C. P., Teo, Y. H., & Wong, P. (2003). Creating a conducive learning environment for the effective integration of ICT: classroom management issues. *Journal of Interactive Learning Research, 14*(4), 405–423.

Cuthbertson, W., & Falcone, A. (2014). Elevating engagement and community in online courses. *Journal of Library & Information Services in Distance Learning, 8*(3–4), 216–224. http://dx.doi.org/10.1080/1533290X.2014.945839.

Deemer, K. (2007). Making the most of the one-shot you got. *Community & Junior College Libraries, 14*(1), 21–26. http://dx.doi.org/10.1300/J107v14n01_04.

Ellison, A. B. (2004). Positive faculty/librarian relationships for productive library assignments. *Community & Junior College Libraries, 12*(2), 23–28. http://dx.doi.org/10.1300/J107v12n02_05.

Farkas, M. (2012). Click here to engage: classroom response systems ease discussion and assessment. *American Libraries, 43*(3–4), 27.

Farwell, K. (2013). Keeping an online class interesting and interactive. *Distance Learning, 10*, 27–32.

Finley, P., Skarl, S., Cox, J., & VanderPol, D. (2005). Enhancing library instruction with peer planning. *Reference Services Review, 33*(1), 112–122.

Gewirtz, S. (2012). Make your library instruction interactive with poll everywhere: an alternative to audience response systems. *College & Research Libraries News, 73*(7), 400–403.

Given, L. M., & Julien, H. (2003). Faculty-librarian relationships in the information literacy context: a content analysis of librarians' expressed attitudes and experiences. *Canadian Journal of Information and Library Science, 27*(3), 65–87.

Gust, K. J. (2006). Teaching with Tiffany's. *Reference Services Review, 34*(4), 557–569. http://dx.doi.org/10.1108/00907320610716440.

Hanz, K., & Lange, J. (2013). Using student questions to direct information literacy workshops. *Reference Services Review, 41*(3), 532–546. http://dx.doi.org/10.1108/RSR-03-2013-0016.

Hoffman, C., & Goodwin, S. (2006). A clicker for your thoughts: technology for active learning. *New Library World, 107*(9/10), 422–433. http://dx.doi.org/10.1108/03074800610702606.

Holbrook, S. (2014). Being proactive: reduce the chaos of a fixed schedule library class. *Library Media Connection, 32*(4), 40–42.

Hoppenfeld, J. (2012). Keeping students engaged with web-based polling in the library instruction session. *Library Hi Tech, 30*(2), 235–252. http://dx.doi.org/10.5260/chara.12.3.57.

Houlson, V. (2007). Getting results from one-shot instruction. *College & Undergraduate Libraries, 14*(1), 89–108. http://dx.doi.org/10.1300/J106v14n01_07.

Isbell, D., & Broaddus, D. (1995). Teaching writing and research as inseparable: a faculty-librarian teaching team. *Reference Services Review, 23*(4), 51–62.

Jacobs, M. L. (2008). Ethics and ethical challenges in library instruction. *Journal of Library Administration, 47*(3–4), 211–232. http://dx.doi.org/10.1080/01930820802186548.

Julian, S. (2013). Reinventing classroom space to re-energise information literacy instruction. *Journal of Information Literacy, 7*(1), 69–82. http://dx.doi.org/10.11645/7.1.1720.

Kimball, K., & O'Connor, L. (2010). Engaging auditory modalities through the use of music in information literacy instruction. *Reference & User Services Quarterly, 49*(4), 316–319.

Langan, K. A., & Sachs, D. E. (2013). Opening Pandora's stream: piping music into the information literacy classroom. *Public Services Quarterly, 9*(2), 89–109. http://dx.doi.org/10.1080/15228959.2013.785876.

Lê, M.-L. (2012). The use of anonymous pop-quizzes (APQs) as a tool to reinforce learning. *Journal of the Medical Library Association, 100*(4), 316–319.

Litten, A. (2002). We're all in this together: planning and leading a retreat for teaching librarians. *Journal of Library Administration, 36*(1/2), 57–69.

MacAdam, B. (1985). Humor in the classroom: implications for the bibliographic instruction librarian. *College & Research Libraries, 46*(4), 327–333. http://dx.doi.org/10.5860/crl_46_04_327.

Mayer, J., & Bowles-Terry, M. (2013). Engagement and assessment in a credit-bearing information literacy course. *Reference Services Review, 41*(1), 62–79. http://dx.doi.org/10.1108/00907321311300884.

Murphy, K. (2010). Is my teaching disturbing you? Strategies for addressing disruptive behaviors in the college classroom. *Journal of Physical Education, Recreation & Dance, 81*(6), 33–37, 44.

Oakleaf, M., Hoover, S., Woodard, B., Corbin, J., Hensley, R., Wakimoto, D., et al. (2012). Notes from the field. *Communications in Information Literacy, 6*(1), 5–23.

Ojala, M. (2013). Business videos. *Online Searcher, 37*(6), 68–70.

Oswald, T. A., & Turnage, M. (2000). First five minutes. *Research Strategies, 17*(4), 347–351. http://dx.doi.org/10.1016/S0734-3310(01)00053-2.

Øvern, K. M. (2014). Faculty-library collaboration: two pedagogical approaches. *Journal of Information Literacy, 8*(2), 36–55. http://dx.doi.org/10.11645/8.2.1910.

Reading, J. (2002). Learning resources and teachers: a discussion of some ideas arising from a research project. *Education Libraries Journal, 45*(1), 13–16.

Ricker, A. S. (1998). Chemistry information for the undergraduate in a one-credit course. *Science & Technology Libraries, 16*(3–4), 45–67. http://dx.doi.org/10.1300/J122v16n03_04.

Sacks, D. (1996). Breathing new life into ancient Greece and Rome. *School Library Journal, 42*, 38–39.

Saunders, L. (2002). Teaching the library: best practices. *Library Philosophy and Practice, 4*(2). Retrieved from http://go.galegroup.com.ezproxylocal.library.nova.edu/ps/i.do?id=GALE%7CA128607098&v=2.1&u=novaseu_main&it=r&p=AONE&sw=w&asid=1769453984fd560dca2889c8989cee68.

Schoofs, B. (2010). Voice in teaching: improving your classroom connection. *College & Research Libraries News, 71*(3), 143–144.

School Library Monthly. (2011). Classroom management. *School Library Monthly, 28*(1), 30.

Scripps-Hoekstra, L. (2013). Eight tips from the trenches: how experience teaching high school informs my approach to information literacy instruction. *College & Research Libraries News, 74*(5), 252–253.

Shamchuk, L., & Plouffe, L. (2013). MacEwan University Library's pedagogical shift: using active learning activities during first-year information literacy sessions. *College & Research Libraries News, 74*(9), 480–495.

Sinkinson, C., & Alexander, S. (2008). Providing the right instructional development opportunities, *34*(4), 4–10.

Springer, A., & Yelinek, K. (2011). Teaching with the situation: "Jersey Shore" as a popular culture example in information literacy classes. *College & Research Libraries News, 72*(2), 78–118.

Sullivan, R. (2014). The iPad in library instruction: collaborative inquiry for information retrieval. *College & Undergraduate Libraries, 21*(2), 232–238. http://dx.doi.org/10.1080/10691316.2014.906794.

Tewell, E. C. (2014). What stand-up comedians teach us about library instruction: four lessons for the classroom. *College & Research Libraries News, 75*(1), 28–30.

Trefts, K., & Blakeslee, S. (2000). Did you hear the one about the boolean operators? Incorporating comedy into library instruction. *Reference Services Review, 28*(4), 369–377.

Vander Meer, P. F., Ring, D. M., & Perez-Stable, M. A. (2007). Engaging the masses: library instruction with large undergraduate classes. *College and Undergraduate Libraries, 14*(1), 39–56. http://dx.doi.org/10.1300/J106v14n01_04.

Vossler, J., & Sheidlower, S. (2001). *Humor and information literacy: Practical techniques for library instruction.* Santa Barbara, CA: Libraries Unlimited.

Walker, B. E. (2006). Using humor in library instruction. *Reference Services Review, 34*(1), 117–128. http://dx.doi.org/10.1108/00907320610648806.

Walker, B. E. (2008). This is jeopardy! An exciting approach to learning in library instruction. *Reference Services Review, 36*(4), 381–388. http://dx.doi.org/10.1108/00907320810920351.

Walker, K. W., & Pearce, M. (2014). Student engagement in one-shot library instruction. *The Journal of Academic Librarianship, 40*(3–4), 281–290. http://dx.doi.org/10.1016/j.acalib.2014.04.004.

Willis, C. N., & Thomas, W. J. (2006). Students as audience: identity and information literacy instruction. *Portal: Libraries and the Academy, 6*(4), 431–444.

Zdravkovska, N., Cech, M., Beygo, P., & Kackley, B. (2010). Laser pointers: low-cost, low-tech innovative, interactive instruction tool. *The Journal of Academic Librarianship, 36*(5), 440–444. http://dx.doi.org/10.1016/j.acalib.2010.06.008.

Zhang, W. (2001). Building partnerships in liberal arts education: library team teaching. *Reference Services Review, 29*(2), 141–149.

CHAPTER 5

Practical Tips for Successful One-Shot Instruction

5.1 ADVICE FROM OTHER ACADEMIC LIBRARIANS

When preparing for any instruction session, spend some time thinking about how you will engage students before and during the session. Downey, Ramin, and Byerly (2008) suggest rearranging the classroom to better facilitate discussion, talking informally with students as they arrive, which should include communicating that you expect participation. During the session, provide nonthreatening opportunities for everyone to participate, but be sure to give students time to think when asking questions. When students answer questions, reward them with praise or small treats. Try to reduce anonymity by asking students about their previous experiences in the library and draw students into the discussion by making eye contact with those students that look interested. Also, remember to allow time for informal questions and answers at the end of the session. When conducting one-shot library instruction sessions specifically, Woodard (Oakleaf et al., 2012) offers some more practical advice. When teaching students about searching for articles, try to balance the students' experience in searching, or work through an example with them and help them to think of general concepts from personal observations. Ask them questions about adding more synonyms using Boolean operators, and what happens when you do so. Ask the students to determine if this results in more or fewer articles. Encourage them to do more searches with the strategy they have just developed, which allows them to see that doing it on their own helps them to retain the skills for future research.

For those who prefer not to improvise their presentation and welcome advice for planning instruction sessions, Corbin (Oakleaf et al., 2012) suggests estimating the amount of time each activity will take.

The Fortuitous Teacher
ISBN 978-0-08-100193-6

When incorporating a new concept or activity you may have to guess, but it is worthwhile to take the time to think about it. If one aspect of the session seems to dominate the entire session, this is a sign that the time allotted for each section may need to be rethought. Tracking the time for each section helps to determine how many learning outcomes can actually fit into the time available. Having a colleague time each section of the lesson plan as he or she observes you is extremely useful. In addition, for each learning outcome you can include details about what you hope students will learn and how you will know they have learned them. Depending on the teaching strategy, you can have a list of examples to demonstrate, or a note to yourself to make sure that students understand the directions provided for the activity they will complete. If you are building the assessment into the activity, include a list of what will provide evidence that the students have learned the concept, for example, correctly filling in a worksheet or the ability to correctly answer a series of questions. You can also simply ask students if they have questions about what they just learned before moving to the next part of the lesson. Keep in mind that when adding student-centered active learning to instruction sessions you should always consider how much class time you spend talking versus that for the students. If there is very little student-centered time, you may consider adding active-learning strategies to your sessions. Although this may seem challenging at first, starting with simple techniques is a good way to start (Downey et al., 2008).

For more advanced techniques think about incorporating technology to improve, extend, and elevate instruction. This is best achieved by knowing the most appropriate time to use technology in library instruction. Keep in mind that not every session needs to be technology integrated, however technology can be used to improve the weaker areas of a lesson plan. In addition, a variety of learning styles can be satisfied by combining visuals and audio through programs such as Audacity, and, specifically, kinesthetic learning with drawing programs like TuxPaint or interactive whiteboards. In general, technology should be used to improve your weaker areas, while being careful not to diminish your strong ones. More than simply adding a

PowerPoint or video to an existing lesson, effective technology integration should enhance those lessons to address a variety of learning styles, extend learning beyond the library, and increase productivity and participation (Ruffin, 2014).

Technology can be used to incorporate games into instruction sessions. Leach and Sugarman (2005) discuss some of the benefits of using games during instruction sessions. Simply put, games engage students in learning. The relaxed, nonthreatening environment created by the use of games helps to encourage student participation. They allow students to review and reinforce the subject matter. Games also address additional learning styles, in that a student who has difficulty retaining information presented during the lecture may have more success in learning information concepts when their classmates are giving answers, or when they are a part of a team answering questions. They may more easily understand information presented in a visual format than in the auditory format of a lecture or a hands–on activity. When designing the game, be sure to base it on learning outcomes, so that it reinforces the information covered in the instruction session and can be used to evaluate what the students learned. Games provide instruction librarians with valuable feedback to modify and improve future instruction sessions. This may mean using an alternate teaching strategy, incorporating analogies that help students understand a concept more easily, or restructuring the entire session. It is always best to keep games simple, for instance, if the librarian chooses the questions rather than allowing the students to do so, the pace of the game is more easily controlled, and the activity can be completed in a much shorter time. However, be prepared for the unexpected when using games in a class session. Keep in mind that each class has different needs and challenges, and it is essential to maintain a constructive learning environment. From a marketing perspective, the use of games in the classroom helps to change the image of librarians from unapproachable and inflexible, to welcoming and fun loving. The students and the librarian can interact in a relaxed and entertaining way if instruction is presented in a lively and fresh manner. Moreover, if the last activity of the instruction session is a game, the students are more likely to leave with a positive impression of the entire experience.

Just as the use of games in library instruction has increased tremendously, so has the use of web-based polling systems. Hoppenfeld (2012) has found that polling systems are a great time-saver compared to paper-based surveys that require time to hand out, collect, and track. These polling systems also save money, because most web-based polling systems are usually free, compared to Clicker polling systems which are not. Clicker systems provide only one option for polling, whereas online polling systems provide multiple options for the audience to respond. Answers can usually be submitted via a website, on Twitter, or via text message. Students have the option of using a computer or their phones to submit their answers. Poll Everywhere, a popular web-based polling site is a good example of how these systems provide a certain freedom in the classroom environment. With just an Internet connection and a projector, the audience can view the results of a poll as they are compiled.

The use of technology with students is commonly associated with younger undergraduates. Kipnis and Childs (2004) offer specific tips for instruction librarians who need to meet the changing generational needs of their patrons. They discuss specific generational qualities and attitudes of Generation X and Generation Y along with educational techniques and software recommendations. Both Generation X and Generation Y grew up with computer games, television, and multimedia presentations, so providing documentation that is text heavy does not work well for these students. Text-based presentations are less popular than those which use a variety of images, including screen shots and step-by-step instructions. Start the workshop by not only introducing yourself, but also mentioning your background including your qualifications. This will let students know that you are a capable, experienced teacher with a fitting educational background. After introducing yourself, give a clear overview of the session and how the lesson is relevant to them. Using humor in a presentation is always a positive, and the more current the humor, the better. Irony also tends to work well, as well as self-deprecating humor. When addressing students, honesty is refreshing; for example, if you do not know the answer to a question, let them know that you will investigate, and get back to the class later. With this generation, relationship building works best versus hierarchical structures. So although you need to establish your authority, remember to invite participation and display empathy. Think about allowing the students to address you by your first name, however, in more formal class settings you may want to refer to yourself as Professor or Librarian while maintaining a welcoming environment (Kipnis & Childs, 2004).

Be aware that both generations have a great interest in customized products and services, such as those which allow students to create news and auto-alerts in databases. This type of customization allows students to have more control over their searches. Both generations of students seek out others who share their own values. They tend to work well together, so group assignments are a good opportunity to take advantage of this strength. They also tend to be indifferent to rules and regulations and view flexibility as a positive, so allowing students to choose or define a segment of an assignment works well (Kipnis & Childs, 2004).

5.2 CREATING SUCCESSFUL ONE-SHOT INSTRUCTION SESSIONS

The goal of an instruction librarian is to create library sessions that are successful for all of those involved, whether students, faculty, or themselves. Hunt and Birks (2004) recommend using Association of College and Research Libraries (ACRL) best practices for Information Literacy (IL) as a solid foundation from which to build one-shot instruction sessions. Instruction librarians should have goals and objectives that align with those of individual programs, departments, and the institution as a whole. A good way to ensure that this takes place is through close collaboration between the library and discipline-based faculty during the planning and teaching of instruction sessions. In this way, IL skills are taught and developed in context, and students can apply those skills to practical situations. In general, collaboration serves several purposes, fostering the sharing of ideas and expertise, while providing opportunities for exposure to different learning theories and instructional techniques. At the same time, colleagues become familiarized with the subject matter of other scholarly fields. Most importantly, students benefit by learning through different teaching styles and educational approaches. Moreover, when multiple instruction methods are used, assessment of student outcomes in IL is more effective. Continuous assessment allows students to be aware of their development at all stages of the learning process (Hunt & Birks, 2004).

As always, good preparation is essential for creating successful instruction sessions. When preparing for instruction sessions librarians must consider the physical and psychological needs of students, as well as their own. Some librarians fall into the trap of believing that they are so familiar with the lesson content that they do not have to prepare for the lecture in advance. Instead, they attempt to improvise during the session, possibly with the hope that this approach will lead to a more relaxed presentation which will encourage discussion. However, even seasoned public speakers have moments of crisis when they freeze or forget what they planned to say. To avoid this situation, write out a script for the presentation and practice it in front of a colleague or friend. Preparing notes or an outline to refer to during the presentation also helps to avoid instruction crises of this sort (Saunders, 2002).

Preparation can also include ensuring, in advance, that the room and equipment is operational. If the room is available beforehand, spend some time in the room prior to the presentation, using the time to locate lights and equipment controls. Experiment with lighting and equipment, especially if using PowerPoint or other screen projections during the presentation. Practice with the equipment in the room, and know how to set up, turn on, and restart any equipment that will be used during the presentation. It is also a good idea to have a backup plan just in case the equipment malfunctions on the day of the presentation. For instance, backup transparent overheads of PowerPoint slides can be prepared ahead of time to replace the software if needed. Once the technical issues of instruction have been planned and prepared for, instruction librarians can focus on the major element of instruction which is the style or method of teaching to be used. When developing instruction sessions, think about the different learning styles and motivations of students, as well as the techniques and training methods that will best suit their needs (Saunders, 2002).

Consider using ADDIE (Analysis, Design, Development, Implementation, Evaluation), an instructional design model that has become the foundation of many other forms of instructional design. The ADDIE model was created in the 1970s for the US military to help facilitate training efforts. Since that time, the ADDIE model has been modified and adapted several times; however, the underlying framework of ADDIE has always been maintained. One of the main factors contributing to the longevity of the ADDIE model is its adaptability to most, if not all, instructional design. ADDIE is also adaptable to a wide range of educational settings from elementary through postsecondary curriculum. Instruction librarians can easily adapt or customize the generic ADDIE model for incorporating new technologies into a library instruction program. Using the general framework of ADDIE for this purpose would necessitate slight modifications to the individual steps; however, the model would retain its primary design principles (Campbell, 2014).

Once the librarian is fully prepared to teach the instruction session, it can be conducted with this framework in mind. Dewald (1999) discusses several characteristics of conducting successful library instruction sessions. Always clarify the objectives of the instruction, which provides students with context, and an overview of what to expect during the session. Objectives also help the librarian to develop the session. Effective library instruction not only teaches mechanics, but also concepts, so that students can apply the skills they learn to their future research needs. Keep in mind that library instruction is most well received when it is closely aligned to the course and assignment. Students tend to be more receptive to library instruction when they can see that it will immediately benefit the course work and assignments at hand. Presenting information in more than one medium is also helpful to students. Some students learn very well through auditory means, such as a lecture, whereas other students learn best through visual demonstration. Yet other students may benefit from receiving information through both visual and auditory channels. Put into practice, auditory lectures can be supplemented by online visual demonstrations. In this way, the two media are more effective together, than when presented alone. Librarians should aim to structure the sessions around active-learning tasks, which are more beneficial to students than lectures alone. This can be accomplished through individual or group exercises, verbal questioning by the librarian, or any form of practice which reinforces the instruction. For example, small-group exercises have students working together to assist each other in learning to use resources such as indexes, data-bases, or the online catalog. They have the opportunity to discuss questions that do not have a single, definitive answer. Collaborative group learning provides a great opportunity for the instruction librarian to step back, while encouraging the students to develop critical thinking and group problem-solving skills together. Finally, effective library instruction does not conclude with the class session, but gives students the option of asking the librarian for help in the future. This allows students to digest, practice, and reflect on their new skills; and if necessary return to the librarian with further questions.

Incorporating games is another important element of creating successful library instruction sessions today, especially at the under-graduate level. Broussard (2012) offers six recommendations for incorporating games into library instruction. It is important to keep games simple, from their design to their use. Although the game may not be very technically impressive, or graphically appealing, in the library instruction session simple games tend to be the most successful. Incorporate the game within the lesson plan so that you can capitalize on its social benefits; for example, online games can allow students to work in groups. Integrating the game's activities can also demonstrate the content of a lesson plan. Use "gating," an in-game device that prevents players from progressing before they have mastered a skill related to key concepts. Gating prevents players from missing skills or clues that will be critical to their progress in higher levels, when they would be frustrated beyond their abilities. Remember to make the game fun, which can easily be achieved by including a fictional story line. Fantasy is an important element of games, and incorporating the rules into the story allows players to learn them as they play. The stronger the link between the story and the game's activities, the stronger will be the context for learning. Provide students with abundant feedback during the game. If it is constant and immediate, it will leave them with a great sense of accomplishment. Reward players after they have successfully completed each level. In addition, badges can be used to reward the student who completes each individual level the best, the fastest, or with the most comments. This allows several additional players to be winners, along with the overall winning student. Moreover, be sure to conduct an assessment, called "playtesting" in the game industry. Playtesting should be a part of the game's early development and, of course, continue once it is put into use.

When incorporating active-learning strategies, games, or otherwise, Hanz and Lange (2013) recommend the following best practices. Carefully weigh the amount of time you have for the number of students participating in the activity. Keep in mind that, with larger classes, an activity may be difficult to orchestrate, and students may benefit from working in pairs. Try asking the students challenging questions, which are a great opportunity for instruction, for instance, to make the students aware of various branch libraries, or the variety of subject materials available at the university library. Remember that when asking students to participate in an activity, there is always the chance that they will not cooperate. For this reason, it is a good idea to prepare a backup presentation, just in case the planned activity does not garner student participation.

The flipped classroom model incorporates elements of active learning. When using this model for one-shot instruction sessions, Datig and Ruswick (2013) provide the following advice. Be willing to experiment in a creative way, making sure that students are actually completing the activities outside of the classroom beforehand. This increases the effectiveness of the technique exponentially, and raises the level of class discussion. Student motivation can also be increased by employing short, in-class quizzes, or requiring quick presentations on the readings. Ask faculty to make completion of the out-of-classroom activities a part of the students' grades. In general, greater collaboration with faculty may provide good feedback on the effectiveness of these strategies over the long term. Collaboration allows instruction librarians to develop stronger skill sets and ideas for conducting class sessions. It also helps them to be willing to give up some control and authority over the classroom.

All of these tips can be applied to online instruction sessions. However, when designing online sessions, librarians should remember that their distance audience is going to be very diverse, being sure to include accessibility features for students with disabilities, and keeping different learning styles in mind. Catalano (2014) gives the following tips which can be applied to online one-shot sessions. Provide the instructional content in multiple formats, for example, a tutorial about finding databases can be accompanied by a printable handout with instructions and visuals. Give instructions on how to use any new technologies, remembering that students have varying skill levels. For their convenience, provide links to free screen readers and audio for lectures. Ensure that all materials are made accessible, including alternative text (alt tags) and captions for video clips. In addition, be sure to include a statement directing students to the university office which provides services for disabled students.

5.3 ASSESSMENT: BUILDING ON SUCCESS

Eduscapes at http://eduscapes.com/instruction/index.htm encourages instruction librarians to consider two types of formal assessment: formative and summative. Formative assessment occurs during the instructional experience to gauge what students are learning. It involves observing student participation in discussion and activities in class. The instructors are usually able to discover if students have completed assigned reading and assignments by observing small-group discussions or asking for in-class responses to reading questions. They are used to provide feedback to the learner about their progress and to adjust instructional materials to improve the learning experience (Lamb, 2015). Formative evaluation is useful in the development of materials, through revision and improvement. Practice exercises, classroom response systems, and student reflections can all be used as part of formative assessment. For example, students are given an information source such as book, periodical article, or website, with the objective of correctly identifying the citation elements for each format. Putting this into practice during an instruction session, students move from station to station in the classroom working with each of six different items representing different formats. For each item, they are instructed to make selections from a list of citation elements (Mayer & Bowles-Terry, 2013).

It is important to note that formative assessment is not a single assessment; rather, formative assessment involves a series of activities in which instructors or students or both use assessment-based evidence to adjust their teaching or learning. The use of assessments is central to the process of eliciting evidence regarding the degree to which a particular student has mastered a particular skill; however, the assessments alone do not represent the formative assessment process. Formative assessment refers to a process, rather than to a particular assessment tool. Formative assessment involves instructional activities that are currently in progress; therefore, instructors' modifications to instructional activities must focus on students' mastery of the skills or concepts currently being pursued. Data from assessments conducted as part of the formative assessment process are used to adjust instruction that is in progress. Assessment is the first part of the formative assessment process; the second part of this process involves instructors' use of assessment results to adjust ongoing instruction activities. Along with in-session assessment questions, pre-assessment exercises can be used to evaluate students' existing IL skills and to adjust the content of the instruction session accordingly (Dunaway & Orblych, 2011).

Dunaway and Orblych (2011) propose that the use of assessments to inform instruction increases the practicality of research instruction. The use of formative assessment creates effective IL instruction by acknowledging variation in IL skills among students. At the University of Michigan–Dearborn Mardigian Library, a librarian worked with a faculty member to create library instruction sessions for business courses at the graduate level. Students were given an open-ended preassessment exercise prior to the session, and their responses were used to determine what the instruction session would cover. Through the assessment questions administered during the session the librarian was given a measure of how the preassessment exercise impacted students' IL skills, gave students feedback regarding their individual IL skills and helped to engage students during the learning process. Together, the preassessment exercise and the in-session questions helped to create an instruction session with content that was appropriate for the students. In this way, these IL instruction sessions were more practical and beneficial to the students than sessions based only on predetermined content.

Summative assessment is a final check of student performance used to determine whether objectives have been reached. This might include a standardized test, final exam, survey, or reflection. Summative evaluation is used to assess instruction after it has been conducted. Bryan and Karshmer (2013) showed how pre- and posttests can be used to gauge student learning, with pre- and posttest assessment specifically within the one-shot instruction model. The use of pretests enables researchers to establish a baseline level of knowledge and determine, by comparison to the posttest results, whether the instructional design produced the desired results. The pre- and posttest comparison had two objectives. First, it compared the overall level of library skills before and after receiving library instruction. Second, it determined if the integration of nonlinguistic representations into the lesson was effective in enhancing student learning. The study explored the effectiveness of using specific nonlinguistic representations, such as kinesthetic, graphic, and physical models, in one-shot library sessions for first-year university students. As suspected, the findings suggest that the use of such representations can enhance student learning and assist in developing research proficiency that are essential to acquiring IL skills.

Instruction librarians should strive to employ a variety of assessment methods to accurately measure student learning. These methods serve a variety of different purposes, provided they are used appropriately. The goal of Carter (2013) was to share one very practical form of authentic assessment crafted for one-shot library instruction sessions. This method does not require an extensive amount of time or work and, in fact, allows the librarians to use the resources most available to them. It allows for the transformation of an existing active learning module or in-class activity into an assessment. By focusing on the evaluation of ACRL outcomes, the building blocks of performance indicators and standards, librarians can accurately get to the root of teaching and learning issues. In turn, improvements can be made, and librarians will successfully close the loop. The main purpose of this assessment method aimed to provide immediate feedback following one-shot instruction sessions, specifically gauging how student's learned to identify keywords and synonyms. The instruction librarians taught most instances of this outcome during the first sessions of an English composition class, pairing it with an assignment which asked students to compare and contrast two sources. Results of the worksheets showed that most students successfully identified keywords within their topics or research questions, as well as chose appropriate synonyms and related terms for the keywords. Minor adjustments to teaching techniques would be expected to correct any weaknesses in the results. These issues were communicated to other teaching librarians along with suggestions of ways to remedy the concerns and ensure that all of the students gain the necessary skills. Carter's practical approach shares formative, authentic assessment of ACRL outcomes within individual sessions of course-integrated IL. The focus is placed on a specific ACRL outcome at the individual-session level. This method does not necessitate extra class time and assists librarians in modifying their teaching techniques to improve student learning. It provides a realistic means of assessing student learning outcomes. Due to the popularity of active learning, many librarians should already have in-class activities that they could easily convert into assessments (Carter, 2013).

Assessment can also be a useful tool for aligning librarian priorities and preexisting student skills. Librarians can work collaboratively to evaluate the results of the assessment and determine the implications for the session goals and objectives. Assessment can be used to determine what skills students already possessed as entering first-year students, to define appropriate goals and objectives for library instruction sessions occurring in first-year composition courses. A pretest can be administered during the first 2 weeks of the fall semester. After the one-shot library instruction, students can take a posttest during the final exam period of that fall semester. In Swoger (2011), librarians found that the original goals and objectives for the library instruction sessions were out of sync with student skills. Assessment also revealed that the original goals and objectives were out of sync with librarian priorities. It suggests that instruction librarians should include evaluation of course goals and objectives as part of the assessment cycle.

Librarians at the University of North Texas developed Library Instruction Software for Assessment (LISA) to assess one-shot library instruction sessions. They conducted an empirical study to demonstrate the value of one-shot instruction assessment and student learning with the software. The study used a pretest, a posttest, and a post-posttest to test freshmen in English classes. The pretest revealed that students had difficulty using some tools more than others, for instance, the library catalog. The posttest showed that student performance searching the catalog and Academic Search Premier improved with library instruction. However, students' ability to find the "Help page" decreased. This decreased number was attributed to the importance of teaching navigation skills in library instruction sessions. The post-posttest taken at the end of the semester demonstrated that students were retaining the skills they had been taught. This study showed that one-shot library instruction sessions are valuable and can be assessed using the LISA software. It also shows that LISA can provide meaningful results about students' library skills (Byerly, Downey, & Ramin, 2006).

Instruction librarians developed an information evaluation activity used in one-shot library instruction for English composition classes (Radom & Gammons, 2014). Researchers modified the "Five Ws" (who, what, when, etc.) to create a formative assessment that introduced evaluation skills to students and piloted it in fall 2011 during one-shot library instruction sessions for English composition classes. Full implementation followed in fall 2012. In both the pilot and the formal study, a summative assessment was sent to students about 3 weeks after the library session to assess their recall and application of the evaluation method. Composition instructors were also surveyed to assess their responses to the Five Ws evaluation method and determine whether they had added, or would consider adding, the method to their own instruction. The findings of these assessments may be relevant to instruction librarians and composition instructors, as well as those interested in the connections between IL competencies and student learning outcomes in general education. The activity guided students through evaluation using the Five Ws method of inquiry. A summative assessment determined student recall and application of the method. Findings, consistent over two semesters, showed that 66.0% of students applied or recalled at least one of the Five Ws, and 20.8% of students applied or recalled more than one of its six criteria. Instructors were also surveyed, with 100% finding value in the method, and 83.3% using or planning to use it in their own teaching.

Generally, evaluation of one-shot instruction is seen as challenging due to the very brief contact with students during that single session. Despite these potential challenges, librarians at the Hong Kong University of Science and Technology (HKUST) made their first attempt at a formal assessment of the library instruction program by conducting a survey of library class attendees in 2004. The results demonstrate the value of the program and provide insights for improvement. They found the survey results encouraging and insightful. It also affirmed the value of the library classes and provided some useful suggestions for program development. Analysis of the results showed that most attendees agreed that the library class had helped them, and many continued to use the skills learned after the delay period. Based on the suggestions from the survey, HKUST librarians have taken steps to improve their classes. Most librarians reconsidered the length of the sessions and the content of their handouts. For instance, one librarian reduced the length of a Master of Business Administration (MBA) class from 80 to 60 min. Another librarian split a large class of 60 students into two groups so that each student could benefit from hands-on practice (Wong, Chan, & Chu, 2006).

Warner (2003) describes efforts at Rider University Libraries to improve their library instruction program by identifying and responding to learning problems. A formal pilot assessment was conducted with a group of 48 students enrolled in a summer 2001 prefreshmen program. The intent was to improve the library instruction program by applying what they learned from the pilot to the more typical "one-shot" library instruction sessions. Three assessment tools were introduced: a journal tool (integrated into the assignments), a faculty reflection tool (used by all of the librarians and by the professors), and an assessment of the summer program upperclassmen (all of whom participated in similar assignments during their freshman year). Both the journal tool and the faculty reflection tool assessed all of the ACRL IL Competency Standards for Higher Education. The upperclassmen assessment tool assessed all but the fourth and fifth standards. By using several assessment tools, they were able to compare the results of each. The journal tool was designed to elicit personalized answers, and it provided a clear documentation of student learning. For example, it allowed them to easily determine the effectiveness of the students' search statements. The reflection tool was most effective in promoting dialog between teaching faculty and librarians, which resulted in the revision of the librarians' teaching strategies. It did not serve well as a documentation of overall student learning, but did provide observed examples of the learning experience occurring for individuals within the hands-on sessions. The observation of the students' speeches in the fall allowed the librarians to determine how students incorporated the information from the resources into their speeches.

A group of Alberta, Canada, academic librarians created the Information Literacy Assessment and Advocacy Pilot (ILAAP), a multiphased research project to investigate the IL skills of postsecondary students and build a robust model for assessing the IL skills required for undergraduate student success. The result was the creation of an IL instruction assessment tool that responds to the unique needs of individual institutions and provides a strategic and relevant model for assessing IL skills among undergraduate students. The research team designed a posttest questionnaire comprising two demographic questions, two open-ended questions, and a pool of skill-based multiple-choice questions based on the ACRL IL Competency Standards for Higher Education. Participating librarians used a customized questionnaire to assess student learning at the end of their one-shot instruction sessions. According to their findings, students demonstrated a clear understanding of the ethical use of information and a strong ability to select appropriate tools for accessing information sources. Student responses to the open-ended questions revealed a wide range of confidence and ability levels, and provided insight into the frequency, depth, and breadth with which various ACRL Standards are being addressed in library sessions. Keeping in mind that many academic libraries require this type of assessment process and tool, the ILAAP team was careful to build an analysis of the pilot's progress into the process to determine the potential for ongoing and broader use of the assessment tool. In September 2013, two new institutions in Alberta were invited to start using the ILAAP tool in their IL sessions. This step provided the team with evidence that the tool had broader applicability outside the original four institutions. More formalized validity testing of the questions was planned for the spring of 2014 to make any necessary revisions to the questions. After any revision, the pilot could then be moved to project phase and additional North American academic libraries would be invited to use the tool (Sharun, Thomson, Goebel, & Knoch, 2014).

5.4 WHAT'S NEXT? THE FUTURE OF EFFECTIVE LIBRARY INSTRUCTION

Current trends in library instruction indicate that librarians are continuing to explore different instructional models, expand their influence in online distance education (DE), and take advantage of web 2.0 technologies such as cloud computing, Massive Open Online Courses (MOOCs), and digital badges. They are also looking to different fields such as business and gaming for ways to expand their instructional reach.

One instructional model that has gained popularity is the idea of "flipping the classroom" due to huge advancements in the technology that help to support this teaching style. In the flipped classroom the students do traditional class work at home, for example, view a prerecorded version of the lesson, and then complete what would be considered homework during the class session. This technique is effective mostly because the instructor is present to assist the student and guide the practical application of the material. The flipped-class model is quickly moving to the forefront of current education trends and discussion. Some feel that this relatively novel idea of flipping the classroom may pass away like many other educational fads of the past. However, the main foundation of the concept is firmly grounded in a common teaching practice, which is having the students actively engaged during the class as opposed to passively taking notes while listening to a lecture. This model also takes advantage of new, readily available technologies which are user-friendly and easy for instructors to incorporate when creating instructional content. The technology also makes the lessons easily available to students on various platforms and course management systems. The flipped-classroom model in library instruction enhances the class session and improves student learning by allowing instructors to devote the entire class time to the practice of research. The use of the flipped-classroom model for library instruction should continue to be a very beneficial and effective tool for library instructors (Rivera, 2015).

Just as many educators are using the flipped-classroom model of inverting curriculum delivery, health sciences librarians are beginning to explore the model for library instruction. The flipped-classroom model is taking hold in various health sciences programs, and academic health sciences libraries are investigating the model as one way to provide library instruction. Academic libraries are testing and evaluating the flipped classroom for various types of library instruction. With the increasing use of online learning tools and strategies, the flipped classroom will continue to be explored as a dynamic and appealing model to deliver instruction in higher education and in academic libraries. The flipped-instruction model should not be limited to traditional instructional settings, and the opportunity exists to employ it in a variety of contexts, from informal teaching scenarios, lengthy workshops, outreach events, and reference services. It is recommended that instruction librarians anticipate and plan for difficulties with gaining faculty buy-in, increasing students' comfort level with the model, spending more time inverting instruction, and making sure that flipped content is accessible and complies with the Americans with Disabilities Act (ADA) (Youngkin, 2014).

Instruction librarians are also looking at various business models to promote and enhance library instruction. Most instruction librarians are familiar with the need to gain faculty buy-in simply to have the opportunity to introduce the library's resources to first-year students during one-shot instruction sessions. These sessions can also be used as an opportunity to promote the entire library and its resources to students. Instruction librarians should consider adopting the practices of business and marketing professionals who also depend on one-shot "selling" meetings to convince their target audience to "buy" their wares. Similarly, business presentation techniques can be used in the one-shot library instruction sessions to "sell" the library to students and faculty, resulting in the creation of a loyal return customer. Librarians have adopted methods and techniques from other disciplines, for example, the Direct-Instruction Teaching Model, a model derived from Learning Theory; and the pedagogical theories of literary theorist Brian Cambourne (Masuchika, 2015).

Business models can be employed to help instruction librarians with issues related to presentation anxiety and the excessive use of library jargon. To alleviate these issues instruction librarians simply need to prepare, just as all salespersons prepare. Attempting to convince or persuade an audience is fruitless without adequate preparation. For those librarians who have taught one-shot instruction sessions for many years, it is easy to become complacent, approaching each class in the same way and expecting the same interactions and responses from all students. This static approach can be limiting, not adapting to the inevitable changes in lesson plans, as well as information storage and retrieval technologies. This approach can also be risky if it results in the use of outdated technology when instructing a younger, more technologically savvy group of students. To avoid this instruction librarians are encouraged to speak directly to the faculty member, request the class syllabus, and modify their presentation according to the students' needs. Another technique that instruction librarians can employ is to also ask their more experienced colleagues for advice about in teaching in general or teaching a specific subject. Attending a library session conducted by a more experienced teaching librarian will allow them to learn through observation. Through these and other methods, all librarians can be more prepared and alleviate problems such as their own anxiety and the excessive use of jargon (Masuchika, 2015).

Another arena that instruction librarians can turn to for advice is the gaming industry. Using games during IL instruction is increasing in popularity, and is more accepted. Since the mid-2000s, a substantial amount of literature has been generated on the subject of games in library instruction. Game-based learning in IL instruction is relatively new, compared to nonlibrary educators who have incorporated games into their pedagogy for a far longer time than have librarians. Nondigital games are being implemented at many college and university libraries due to the simplicity of play and their ability to increase personal engagement with others in a class. As early as 1982, the use of digital and online games appeared in college and university library instruction sessions. In one instance, an arcade-style game randomly assigned students one of 10 topics and then required them to construct a bibliography of a predetermined number of sources as quickly as possible using a specific resource. The game's creators found that, when implemented in IL instruction sessions, short online games which address specific research processes, such as identifying keywords and synonyms, can be successfully used to improve students' understanding of those skills (Tewell & Angell, 2015).

These early game technologies, in part, have led to instruction librarians being at the forefront of adopting web 2.0 technologies and later cloud-computing applications. Teaching "in the cloud" has offered new and even more efficient tools for teaching and faculty collaboration. Cooperative learning also tends to be enhanced using cloud-computing applications. Regardless of the discipline or subject matter, learning activities such as discussion, peer review, collaborative writing, team projects, and reflective journals can be pursued online. Cloud-computing tools for creating tutorials and surveys, collaboration, events scheduling, and storage can enhance engagement among students, educators, and researchers in a cost-effective manner (Koury & Jardine, 2013).

Luo (2012) examined how reference librarians use cloud-computing technologies, particularly general-purpose, consumer-oriented software tools, to support and facilitate their work. A survey was conducted and the findings suggest that librarians use these tools for a variety of purposes, ranging from facilitating internal communication and collaborative work, to supporting IL instruction. Some advantages of using these tools are that they are universally accessible, inexpensive, or free, require minimal IT maintenance, are user-friendly, and support collaborative work. Some noted disadvantages were identified, such as Internet dependence, privacy concerns, limitations with free versions, and glitches with open source tools. Instruction librarians interested in the use of cloud computing should first gain a concrete understanding of how to benefit from it so they can make informed decisions when migrating to it.

Another new feature of online education is the MOOC. MOOCs describe online classes that are not only offered on a large scale, but are free and open to the public. Instruction librarians already provide support to formally enrolled higher education students in developing their information and digital literacy skills, and these same skills are required by their MOOC learners. Along with attempting to navigate a variety of platforms, MOOC students are required to find, select, and analyze information during their learning experience. Instruction librarians may consider making themselves and/or specific resources available for MOOC presentations (Gore, 2014). Librarians have been creating a variety of open online resource tools, such as tutorials, screencasts, and videos as the technology has become available. Librarians may consider adding on to this "tool-kit" by developing IL modules that can easily be embedded in MOOCs. The modules would be most useful if they are self-paced and reusable, containing videos, reading materials, as well as assessments (Wu, 2013).

Digital badges are another popular trend in library instruction today. They are a visual symbol of an earned achievement or skill within a course. Digital badges can be used to direct and keep track of competencies within a course or program curriculum. They show what skills students have learned, the criteria students must meet to earn a badge, and provide evidence of students' achievements. They also acknowledge the authority responsible for assessing students' skills. A digital badge is only as significant as its course curriculum and the assessment of how well students have retained it. Badges are simply a tool that helps educators to improve instructional practices rather than the end goal itself. The implementation of badges are most effective when they are incorporated through thoughtful planning that improves pedagogy and instructional design, and also values instructional design over the implementation of the technology. With strong pedagogical design, students show more engagement and remind students of what they have learned. Badges given out simply for fun and novelty will be meaningless and hold little value for most students (Ford, Izumi, Lottes, & Richardson, 2015).

DE is one of the fastest-growing trends of higher education, which has had a major impact on academic libraries and the instructional services they offer. To meet ACRL standards academic libraries have continuously incorporated changes in the way they provide online services and access to digital resources. The rapid rise in the number of DE programs and students has had the greatest impact on how academic libraries provide instructional services to distance students. For example, instead of always traveling to teach students at a distance, librarians now have the option of engaging them online. Traveling to teach distance students has always had its own set of factors to consider, such as logistics, various escalating costs, and uncertainty about the adequacy of an unfamiliar teaching facility. In an effort to make online instruction as efficient as possible, most instruction librarians have integrated web 2.0 technologies, such as LibGuides, chat widgets, RSS feeds, and social networking applications. Another recent type of effort in providing instruction to DE students is via embedded library instruction. Programs such as these allow librarians to meet DE students in their regular online course by embedding IL instruction. Many instruction librarians host webinars and optionally share their desktop computer display at the same time to guide students through search navigation. Providing instruction to distance learners requires the ability to adapt to various instructional modes, forcing instructors to utilize multiple skills, ranging from the use of technology to online classroom management. Above all, they must be able to convert instructional materials into a format appropriate to the online environment and to communicate the information in a very different medium (Li, 2013). Online course design teams typically consist of an instructor, facilitator, designer, and subject matter expert. Although online course designers do not always consider instruction librarians during the design process, embedded librarians can be valuable members of the instructional design team. They can assist in the development of the course, ensuring that IL concepts are included from the start. As experts in research and technology, instruction librarians have the ability to guide the design process by aligning research projects and assignments with library services and resources (Mudd, Summey, & Upson, 2015).

Whether online or face-to-face, studies seem to indicate that one-shot instructional sessions do not fulfill the IL needs of students, as well as suggest that student engagement cannot be effectively driven by one-shot library instruction alone (Walker & Pearce, 2014). However, given the ongoing prevalence of this instructional format, instruction librarians have no choice but to find ways to ensure that IL concepts become integrated, so students are effectively engaged now and in the future. Incorporating examples of popular culture from television or movies into one-shot instruction sessions have been shown to increase students' understanding of IL concepts (Tewell, 2014). The latest instructional models, technology, and communication techniques are the most effective tools that instructional librarians will utilize to successfully overcome the inevitable challenges of the one-shot instruction session.

REFERENCES

Broussard, M. J. S. (2012). Digital games in academic libraries: a review of games and suggested best practices. *Reference Services Review, 40*(1), 75–89. http://dx.doi.org/10.1108/00907321211203649.

Bryan, J. E., & Karshmer, E. (2013). Assessment in the one-shot session: using pre- and post-tests to measure innovative instructional strategies among first-year students. *College & Research Libraries, 74*(6), 574–586. http://dx.doi.org/10.5860/crl12-369.

Byerly, G., Downey, A., & Ramin, L. (2006). Footholds and foundations: setting freshmen on the path to lifelong learning. *Reference Services Review, 34*(4), 589–598. http://dx.doi.org/10.1108/00907320610716477.

Campbell, P. C. (2014). Modifying ADDIE: incorporating new technologies in library instruction. *Public Services Quarterly, 10*(2), 138–149. http://dx.doi.org/10.1080/15228959.2014.904214.

Carter, T. M. (2013). Use what you have: authentic assessment of in-class activities. *Reference Services Review, 41*(1), 49–61. http://dx.doi.org/10.1108/00907321311300875.

Catalano, A. (2014). Improving distance education for students with special needs: a qualitative study of students' experiences with an online library research course. *Journal of Library & Information Services in Distance Learning, 8*(1–2), 17–31. http://dx.doi.org/10.1080/1533290X.2014.902416.

Datig, I., & Ruswick, C. (2013). Four quick flips: activities for the information literacy classroom. *College & Research Libraries News, 74*(5), 249–257.

Dewald, N. H. (1999). Transporting good library instruction practices into the web environment: an analysis of online tutorials. *Journal of Academic Librarianship, 25*(1), 26–31. http://dx.doi.org/10.1016/S0099-1333(99)80172-4.

Downey, A., Ramin, L., & Byerly, G. (2008). Simple ways to add active learning to your library instruction. *Texas Library Journal, 84*(2), 52–54.

Dunaway, M. K., & Orblych, M. T. (2011). Formative assessment: transforming information literacy instruction. *Reference Services Review, 39*(1), 24–41. http://dx.doi.org/10.1108/00907321111108097.

Eduscapes. (2015). Objectives and Assessments [Webpage]. Retrieved from http://eduscapes.com/instruction/8.htm.

Ford, E., Izumi, B., Lottes, J., & Richardson, D. (2015). Badge it!. *Reference Services Review, 43*(1), 31–44. http://dx.doi.org/10.1108/RSR-07-2014-0026.

Gore, H. (2014). Massive open online courses (MOOCs) and their impact on academic library services: exploring the issues and challenges. *New Review of Academic Librarianship, 20*(1), 4–28. http://dx.doi.org/10.1080/13614533.2013.851609.

Hanz, K., & Lange, J. (2013). Using student questions to direct information literacy workshops. *Reference Services Review, 41*(3), 532–546. http://dx.doi.org/10.1108/RSR-03-2013 -0016.

Hoppenfeld, J. (2012). Keeping students engaged with web-based polling in the library instruction session. *Library Hi Tech, 30*(2), 235–252. http://dx.doi.org/10.1108/07378831211239933.

Hunt, F., & Birks, J. (2004). Best practices in information literacy. *Portal: Libraries and the Academy, 4*(1), 27–39.

Kipnis, D. G., & Childs, G. M. (2004). Educating generation X and generation Y. *Medical Reference Services Quarterly, 23*(4), 25–33. http://dx.doi.org/10.1300/J115v23n04_03.

Koury, R., & Jardine, S. J. (2013). Library instruction in a cloud: perspectives from the trenches. *OCLC Systems & Services: International Digital Library Perspectives, 29*(3), 161–169. http://dx.doi.org/10.1108/OCLC-01-2013-0001.

Lamb, A., (2015). Objectives and Assessment [Webpage]. Retrieved from http://eduscapes.com/instruction/8.htm.

Leach, G. J., & Sugarman, T. S. (2005). Play to win! Using games in library instruction to enhance student learning. *Research Strategies, 20*(3), 191–203. http://dx.doi.org/10.1016/j.resstr.2006.05.002.

Li, P. (2013). Effect of distance education on reference and instructional services in academic libraries. *Internet Reference Services Quarterly, 18*(1), 77–96. http://dx.doi.org/10.1080/10875301.2013.804018.

Luo, L. (2012). Reference librarians' adoption of cloud computing technologies: an exploratory study. *Internet Reference Services Quarterly, 17*(3/4), 147–166. http://dx.doi.org/10.1080/10875301.2013.765824.

Masuchika, G. (2015). Applications of business presentation techniques to one-shot library instruction. *College & Undergraduate Libraries, 22*(1), 61–75. http://dx.doi.org/10.1080/1 0691316.2015.1001243.

Mayer, J., & Bowles-Terry, M. (2013). Engagement and assessment in a credit-bearing information literacy course. *Reference Services Review, 41*(1), 62–79. http://dx.doi. org/10.1108/00907321311300884.

Mudd, A., Summey, T., & Upson, M. (2015). It takes a village to design a course: embedding a librarian in course design. *Journal of Library & Information Services in Distance Learning, 9*(1–2), 69–88. http://dx.doi.org/10.1080/1533290X.2014.946349.

Oakleaf, M., Hoover, S., Woodard, B., Corbin, J., Hensley, R., Wakimoto, D., et al. (2012). Notes from the field. *Communications in Information Literacy, 6*(1), 5–23.

Radom, R., & Gammons, R. W. (2014). Teaching information evaluation with the five ws: an elementary method, an instructional scaffold, and the effect on student recall and application. *Reference & User Services Quarterly, 53*(4), 334–347.

Rivera, E. (2015). Using the flipped classroom model in your library instruction course. *The Reference Librarian, 56*(1), 34–41. http://dx.doi.org/10.1080/02763877.2015.977671.

Ruffin, B. (2014). Library geek feats. *Texas Library Journal, 90*(3), 95–97.

Saunders, L. (2002). Teaching the library: best practices. *Library Philosophy and Practice, 4*(2). Retrieved from http://0-go.galegroup.com.novacat.nova.edu/ps/i.do?id=GALE%7CA 128607098&v=2.1&u=novaseu_main&it=r&p=AONE&sw=w&asid=1769453984fd5 60dca2889c8989cee68.

Sharun, S., Thomson, M. E., Goebel, N., & Knoch, J. (2014). Institutions collaborating on an information literacy assessment tool. *Library Management, 35*(8/9), 538–546. http:// dx.doi.org/10.1108/LM-03-2014-0035.

Swoger, B. J. M. (2011). Closing the assessment loop using pre- and post-assessment. *Reference Services Review, 39*(2), 244–259. http://dx.doi.org/10.1108/00907321111135475.

Tewell, E. C. (2014). Tying television comedies to information literacy: a mixed-methods investigation. *The Journal of Academic Librarianship, 40*(2), 134–141. http://dx.doi.org/ 10.1016/j.acalib.2014.02.004.

Tewell, E., & Angell, K. (2015). Far from a trivial pursuit: assessing the effectiveness of games in information literacy instruction. *Evidence Based Library & Information Practice, 10*(1), 20–33.

Walker, K. W., & Pearce, M. (2014). Student engagement in one-shot library instruction. *The Journal of Academic Librarianship, 40*(3–4), 281–290. http://dx.doi.org/10.1016/j. acalib.2014.04.004.

Warner, D. A. (2003). Programmatic assessment: turning process into practice by teaching for learning. *The Journal of Academic Librarianship, 29*(3), 169–176. http://dx.doi.org/10.1016/ S0099-1333(03)00017-X.

Wong, G., Chan, D., & Chu, S. (2006). Assessing the enduring impact of library instruction programs. *The Journal of Academic Librarianship, 32*(4), 384–395. http://dx.doi. org/10.1016/j.acalib.2006.03.010.

Wu, K. (2013). Academic libraries in the age of MOOCs. *Reference Services Review, 41*(3), 576–587. http://dx.doi.org/10.1108/RSR-03-2013-0015.

Youngkin, C. A. (2014). The flipped classroom: practices and opportunities for health sciences librarians. *Medical Reference Services Quarterly, 33*(4), 367–374. http://dx.doi.org/10.108 0/02763869.2014.957073.

CONCLUSION

The one-shot instruction session remains a fixture in academic libraries today. Academic librarians, seeking to make the most of a single-class session, play many different roles in the instructional design process, from curriculum developer to technical troubleshooter. The one-shot instruction session will likely continue to be the most popular form of library instruction in the future—and librarians will continue to seek practical tips for creating it. This book was written to provide instruction librarians with a practical guide for conducting these sessions, and collaborating with the larger academic community.

I hope that this book provides useful and practical instruction tips. With the continued prevalence of the one-shot instruction session, it is convenient to have a resource which addresses the specific concerns of this type of instruction. By increasing your awareness of the past and present of academic library instruction, while acknowledging the challenges of the one-shot session, this type of instruction will improve.

INDEX

CPI Antony Rowe
Chippenham, UK
2016-05-06 21:08